HOW TO FIND
Love
AND NOT A
PSYCHO

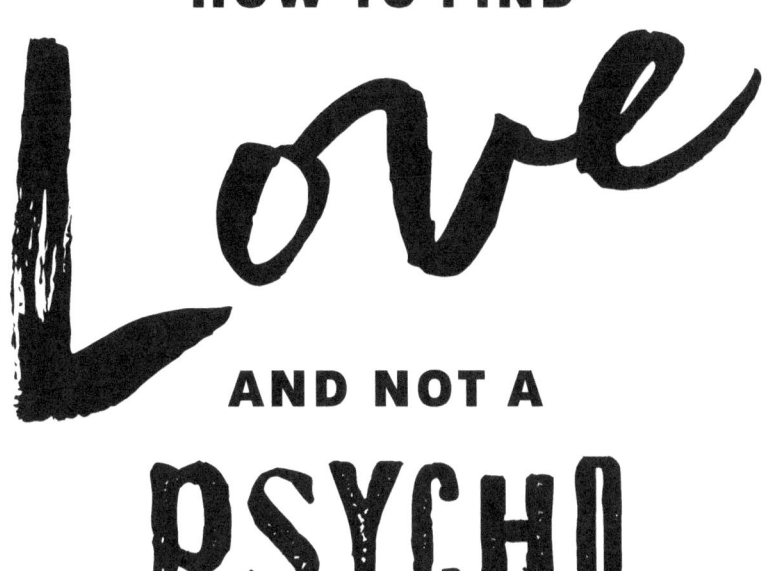

HOW TO FIND Love AND NOT A PSYCHO

DR PHIL WATTS

Copyright 2020 Dr Phil Watts

The moral right of Dr Phil Watts to be identified as the Author of the work has been asserted by him in accordance with the Copyright. Designs and Patents Act 1988. All rights reserved. No part of this book may be used or reproduced, stored in a retrieval system, or transmitted in any form, or by any means electronic, mechanical, recording, photocopying, or in any manner whatsoever without permission in writing from the publisher, except for the inclusions of brief quotations in a review.

A catalogue record for this book is available from the National Library of Australia

ISBN: 978-0-9756042-9-8 Paperback
ISBN: 978-0-9924121-0-4 ebook
Creator: Watts, Phil, 1962- Author
Editing: Linda McNamara
Cover art creative attribution to www.CoverDesignStudio.com and D Sharon Pruitt.
Cover design: Dickson Cheung, Takoprint
Interior and cover layout: Pickawoowoo Publishing Group

Printed & Channel Distribution
Lightning Source | Ingram (USA/UK/EUROPE/AUS)

Dedication

For Jarom and Arielle, my beautiful children, with hope and prayers that they find true love and not a psycho.
To my wife for teaching me why it is worth finding meaningful love.
To all the single people who are looking for someone to make them feel special. It is worth the investment to find the best partner possible.

Contents

Acknowledgements ·ix

How to Find Love and Not a Psycho · · · · · · · · · · · · · · · · · · 1
Use Your Brain · 9
What is Personality?· 17
Personality Disorders· 25
The Best Predictor of Future Behaviour is Past Behaviour · · 35
Before You Buy a Horse, Check Out the Stable · · · · · · · · · · 44
"Aisle" Change Him · 50
The Façade · 56
You Can Get Anything Online · 64
Substance Screen · 70
The Marketplace · 78
Try Before You Buy · 83
The 90% Rule · 90
The No-Test · 96
Finetuning Your Assessment · 102
The Reasonable Person · 108
Getting Out · 114
Mirror, Mirror on the Wall? · 119
The Intimacy Ladder· 125

Assertive Communication · 133
Intimate Partners (Again) · 138
Making it Work · 144
Happily Ever After · 149
After the Affair · 156
I Believe in Love · 162

Acknowledgements

Of all the books I have written this was the most exciting to write! Relationships and break-ups – both mine and those I have observed in the Family Court – have provided me with understanding and ideas for this book. I am grateful to those who have either shared their stories or shared my life to help me understand relationships and, in particular, what can make things go wrong.

The life of an author is somewhat taxing. Writing takes precious time away from those who matter the most in life – a family. I am grateful for my family's support and encouragement. For this reason, the most important acknowledgements are for my beautiful wife Bethwyn, who is my eternal companion, and my children. My wife is an awesome, beautiful and intelligent woman who supports me in all that I do, despite her health problems and the complex difficulties arising from them. I am also inspired to write so that my amazing children, Jarom and Arielle, can see the benefits of having a busy father. As they emerge from their teens, I hope that they will take this book as fatherly advice to help them choose partners with whom to spend their lives.

Most importantly, I would like to acknowledge my typist Sue Tribe who transcribed my spoken words, Linda McNamara who edited and proofread my work, and the staff at Pick-a-WooWoo for helping me to publish this book.

Thanks also to you, the reader, for your interest in this aspect of relationships. I could not think of anything more useful in an adult's life than to be able to understand relationships – to improve the chances of attaining a great relationship with a matching companion.

Dr Phil Watts

How to Find Love and Not a Psycho

Now that the title has caught your attention, I can tell you what this book is really all about. It is about love and relationships. Sometimes we meet people who say that they have been happily married for 30 years and, at other times, we meet people whose relationships have gone bad (as I do in my work as a forensic psychologist). When I say relationships gone bad, I mean seriously bad. Couples who have ripped each other apart. Relationships in which someone is a psychological monster hell-bent on destroying their former lover. Relationships in which there has been physical violence or, more commonly, relationships that are psychologically toxic without the occurrence of a physical incident.

When I forensically interview those people who have experienced these terrible relationships, with the benefit of hindsight they often reveal the warning signs (whether or not they recognise them as such). Little comments are made which I see as flashing warnings like the neon lights in Las Vegas. These signs are frequently neglected by people due to the powerful emotional high associated with love. Oxytocin, the love hormone, dulls our conscious mind from harmful patterns while the joyous rush of love begs us to stay for more. The result is a lack of foresight caused either by a lack of knowledge or the hormonal override. It is for this reason that the expression "love is blind" is still part of modern parlance.

This lack of foresight results in fledgling relationships igniting into turmoil and confusion. The journey is chaotic, traumatic and at times dangerous. Eventually the relationships finish, leaving carnage and wreckage – not just for the couples themselves but sometimes also whole families. Parents, children and grandparents can be dragged into the drama. Dreams smashed. Plates smashed. Problems can continue even after a dramatic relationship collapse. These problems include court battles and conflicts in relation to children and property. The personal toll includes depression and trauma, fear of intimacy, lack of trust and a damaged sense of self.

In the self-reflection stage, you might ask yourself how you got into such a mess. The answer is that some people are master manipulators who can make you believe night is day and that you were at fault. You could be made to feel guilty for not meeting your partner's needs, or you could have been used to fulfil your partner's needs while receiving nothing in return because your partner didn't care about you as a person. The list of possible games is lengthy, and we will revisit some of these themes in due course.

This book has been written for two purposes. The first is to help you avoid making the choices which could land you in that pit of despair described above, so that future stories of bad relationships will refer to others and not to you. I don't want you to be a chapter in my next book. The second purpose is to shed light on the whole process so that you, who can relate to every sad and sorry word above, can recover and not repeat the experience. I also want to help you to not only avoid the true psycho but to make choices which can make a relationship spectacular.

My strong and positive belief is that we are created to have healthy family units which produce effective offspring. We want to be mated pairs in happy families. A good relationship is one of the best places on earth to be. I do not believe that we were designed to be single, which is why we continue to look for a partner. The key to happiness is to ensure that from the start your mate is fundamentally the right one. People can change, but only by degree, not nature. If you want to build a house, it is important to start with the right materials. This book is a do-it-yourself guide to selecting the right building materials.

How great this world would be if we all had a set of tools which helped us see which features make a good companion and, conversely, which features could result in a roller coaster of despair. We could seek the former and avoid people with the latter characteristics. This book is designed to be a tool kit to help you increase the likelihood of identifying those who will chew you up and eventually spit you out, and those who will still make your heart flutter after decades together.

At this stage it is important to clarify that this book is not just about psychos in a particular diagnostic sense. Some dysfunctional relationships are based on seriously ill people with diagnosable conditions. In the following chapters I will specifically address some of these types of people as they can tear lives apart. Fortunately, most people are not like that. For many of us it is about picking someone who is compatible with our beliefs and attitudes, because if you find someone who is different from you it often results in a hard relationship. It's about trying to find a good relationship and avoiding ending up with a partner who, through their conduct, will make your life miserable.

I have spent my career working in family law and as a court expert I have assessed over 1,300 families going through difficult and complex separations. I have had the honour and privilege of listening to 2,600 stories of how people met, what went wrong, and why their relationships were a disaster. Internationally, family courts are the repository of society's most dysfunctional and damaged relationships. Reasonable people can solve their problems without resorting to court proceedings. The Family Court environment captures those relationships with problems and difficulties which are not easily solved. I hear and see the warning signs which were evident but neglected.

Most of the difficulties associated with complex Family Court cases arise from poor choice of partner. An occasional but relatively rare situation is that of a later event triggering the demise of the relationship. Such events can include someone becoming seriously unwell or mentally ill, the loss of a child, or some other terrible life event. The trauma or condition then changes a person and the relationship does not survive. If you are in that situation there is nothing you could have done to prevent it, particularly if it was something that just developed in the relationship. In my opinion, psychologically robust people are better able to cope with trauma and therefore a robust partner is a better choice. As stated earlier, this is a less common situation. In most cases people can usually see with hindsight the warning signs that they had neglected to heed. Generally, the problems stem from who you have chosen to be with rather than from some trauma or event that knocked the wheels off the relationship.

One of the most profound factors I have observed is that the warning signs of a dysfunctional relationship were present either from the beginning or very early in the relationship, but the people involved didn't know how to read the signs. As you read through this book you will discover that there are different ways in which people present themselves that obscures their pathology. However, there are several tests and signs which will allow you to more accurately ascertain whether your partner will make your life heaven or hell. Each chapter concludes with a summary of "love finder tools". These are essentially summaries of those things to do or to look for to help you to make good choices or recognise potentially bad choices. These are your tools.

I would like to reiterate that I believe that a relationship with a close and loving partner is one of the best places on earth. In other words, it can be heaven. However, a relationship with someone whose personality is generally destructive, or destructive to your particular nature, can create a living hell. With certain types of personalities that living hell can escalate with separation and, in more extreme cases, the victim of the rage and blame is never free from the conflict generated by their former lover. Life is therefore miserable with no possible escape.

It is often said that the opposite to love is hate. That is not actually true. The opposite to love is indifference; you no longer care about the other person. Hate is a separate relationship. There are some people who would rather be in a hate relationship than in no relationship at all and, therefore, can make your life a misery. The type of person who makes you the target of hate is also likely to have made your relationship with them exceptionally difficult. As you will discover, the journey to hell did not start like that. This is because the first stage is one of deceptive impression management – they treat you better and make you feel more special than you have ever felt before. We will return to this in later chapters when discussing how impression management colours our judgement.

With the breakdown of the village structure in society, it is much harder to identify a healthy and functional partner because a lot of community information has been lost. We no longer have access to local reference checks. This "personality knowledge" over the lifespan of an individual has been lost. We are therefore starting with complete strangers. This allows sinister characters more latitude to practice their art of deception.

Of course, modern technology has evolved in parallel with the breakdown of the village. An important concept I will describe in more detail later in the book, is how the use of the internet for dating has been a blessing (in that it allows for more opportunities to meet a variety of different people), but also a curse (in that it allows people to create personae or avatars which are either altered or completely false representations of themselves). "Catfishing" is a term which has appeared recently. Internet predators who fabricate online identities and entire social circles to trick people into emotional or romantic relationships is becoming a common phenomenon. It is not only necessary to screen for catfish – I want you to avoid anyone who is a bit fishy.

To get the love you want is a complex process, but the starting point is to find the right material with which to build a relationship. As will be explained later in this book, many of the problems brought by people into a relationship are perpetual problems which don't go away. Before you can see somebody's problems, you have to get past their façade – the games people play, and the distortions made possible through the internet and other electronic media. This is no easy task, so there are several chapters based on this topic.

In my opinion, a fundamental part of being human is the desire to be loved and share your life with somebody who values and respects you. The purpose of this book is to allow you to apply some of what we know from psychological science, forensic psychology, the great research into difficult-to-live-with personalities, together with my experience and observations obtained through dealing with high conflict personalities in the Family Court. Understanding this information will provide you with the power to find the ideal partner and to enter into and maintain a long-lasting and fulfilling relationship (rather than have a short distressing relationship or be trapped in a long-term complex and difficult situation where you battle for years to try and break free).

The only way to do this is to create a tool kit for assessing potential partners. As you develop your love finder tools, you will become equipped to screen your future partners in ways that you may not have considered before. This set of tools will give you the psychological x-ray vision to pierce through the façade and image management to see what lies beneath. Through understanding something about dangerous personalities, you will be able to spot markers of dysfunction early enough to do something about it.

The book also aims to provide some strategies about what you should be looking for, and why that could be important when choosing a partner (that is, a person who will treat you in ways which are psychologically healthy and will enhance your own functioning). Ultimately the choice will be yours alone. You can use the information to assist you to choose a desirable and emotionally supportive partner. Conversely you could ignore the tools and increase your risk of making a wrong choice. This book will not guarantee success, but it will increase the odds in your favour once you know what you are looking for.

As a society we say: "I was falling in love". It is the falling I want you to avoid, not the love. To achieve success in a relationship you have to use your head – not just fall blindly. If you can analyse like a psychologist, and not disappear in a mist of hormone-induced love, you have a chance of lasting success. Therefore, a fitting starting point is to examine how your brain operates and then provide you with some information about how the brain can help you with your choice of partner.

Love Finder Tools:

- While the notion of romantic attraction is wonderful in movies, happily ever after can only come from analysis or good luck. Analysis is an important tool to maximise the probability of a happy long-term outcome. Therefore, it is time to analyse and not romanticise.

Use Your Brain

———∞∞∞———

THE HUMAN BRAIN IS THE most astonishing, amazing and beautiful organ. Did you know that it has more neuron connections than there are stars in the universe? With all due respect to the rapidly growing body of neurological science, our understanding of the brain is still primitive. I consider the study of the brain to be one of the great frontiers of knowledge for this century. For the purposes of this book we only need a very basic understanding for me to make my points.

The following discussion of the brain's structures is important but brief, as the focus of this book is on love and personality. In simple terms, the brain has three main parts relevant to this discussion.

The first of the parts (or first level system) is the brain stem and basic reflex system, an ancient system which controls reflex level responses housed in the core of head. Some writers refer to this lump at the top of the spinal column as the "crocodile brain". This part of the brain keeps us alive and basic human functions of survival are managed. Breathing and heart rate just happen – no conscious thought is required. The following are two illustrations of the survival mechanism: a crocodile does not empathise with its prey; and if the young of almost any creature on earth is attacked its parent responds by attacking the threat.

Prisons, and sometimes the internet, are full of people who operate primarily from their crocodile brain. Most people do not function at this reflex level most of the time, however, some people live in crocodile brain mode. Criminals often act to survive and will do whatever it takes to keep alive. It will become evident very quickly if you date someone who lives in this part of the brain. Usually these people are very damaged and leave a trail of destruction. If you can discover something of their life history, it will be full of markers of problems with both the law and other people.

The second level system in the brain is referred to as the limbic system. This system is an inner brain network of significant parts but, most intriguingly, it has parts which connect widely across the brain. Textbooks in this area discuss systems such as the amygdala (fear centre), hypothalamus (the brain regulator), or cingulate gyrus (obsessiveness and anxiety). They connect to hormone pathways such as dopamine (addiction and pleasure), oxytocin (love feelings) or cortical steroids (brain arousal). These systems turn on when emotions are required. They are the source of pleasure, pain, anger, disgust, fear and other emotions. The key message is that the brain has an interconnected network of feelings which serve important emotional purposes. This network is your emotional brain.

To illustrate the role of the emotional brain, consider the following example. If you cross a road of heavy traffic and a car nearly hits you, in those moments you do not calculate the physics of what is happening (that is, the braking distance of the oncoming car). Instead, almost instantly, a surge of adrenaline fills your body, your heart pounds rapidly with the blood rushing from your gut to your legs and arms, and you jump out of the way. Afterwards your body takes a while to calm down, and the next time you are near that road you will be hypervigilant to avoid repeating the same mistake. The emotional system is quite complex, even for a simple event, but it gets you out of danger very quickly. Bottom line, when emotions are appropriate to the situation, the system is amazingly efficient at ensuring survival by reacting and not thinking.

Unfortunately, sometimes the emotional brain does not work properly. For example, if someone had experienced a trauma the brain might activate but not turn off again. Some people's brains are permanently in a state of arousal, firing up unpredictably due to minor triggers of risk. These people might want to jump out of the way of every car, not just a speeding car. A psychologist might call this anxiety or Post Traumatic Stress Disorder (PTSD) depending upon the cause and exact symptoms. Other people's brains are underactive and do not react when they should. This may be a symptom of autism, or certain types of attachment disorder or personality disorder. A variety of forces can shape how the emotional system operates, but the key factors are genetics, early childhood experiences, and trauma. These factors cause someone to be either normal or extreme in their emotional responses.

The third level system in the brain is the cortex. This is the outer layer of the brain and is the wrinkly looking grey matter. The cortex has several jobs to do, but the primary one is to be the main thinking system. The back of the brain is for vision, and the sides are for memory, language, spatial relationships, mathematics and other abilities. The front part of the brain, the frontal lobes, are really the part of the brain that separates us from other animals and makes us unique. Frontal lobes control our ability to concentrate, focus and stay on task (hence Attention Deficit Hyperactivity Disorder (ADHD) is largely related to the frontal lobe), plan and organise, consider consequences, regulate anger and other emotions, as well as provide links to our personality.

The limbic system is the emotional arousal system, but the frontal lobes are also connected. Studies show that in many respects the frontal lobes are the handbrake to the limbic system. Cognitive control from the frontal lobes calms the emotional systems, which is why mindfulness and cognitive behavioural therapy can help calm emotional conditions. The success of a relationship with someone who has a cortex-based problem will depend upon the location of the problem. If the problem is frontally related, the very things needed for the relationship will already be impaired. Patience, acceptance, problem solving and the ability to learn from mistakes are vital ingredients for a mature and healthy relationship, yet they will not be working under these circumstances. Therefore, it could be disastrous to attempt to have a relationship with someone who is reactive due to frontal lobe issues. Finding someone with good frontal lobes is important, however, it is unlikely that you would send prospective partners to a neuropsychologist for frontal lobe checks. You need work it out for yourself by looking at the person's life patterns.

As a forensic psychologist, I am asked what makes someone do bad things. My tongue-in-cheek answer is that the person could have a problem in the frontal lobes or with attachment. Frontal lobe problems might include damage, ADHD, low IQ or a myriad of other issues which can impact rational thinking. Attachment can include early damage in childhood that puts the emotional brain into reactivity states resulting in instability (this will be discussed in more detail later). The key point with ADHD and other brain-based conditions is whether the condition is being well-managed. Someone with ADHD can make a good partner if they have learnt to manage their impulsivity and reactivity.

My advice is that if you want a good relationship, find good frontal lobes and check out the emotional systems! You don't need to do brain scans, but you need to look for evidence that these systems are working. I know that you would rather check out the other person's physical attributes. Perhaps online dating adverts in the future will include not only "seeks good sense of humour" but "high functioning frontal lobes" as core selling points. I know that would be of interest to me, but I am an enlightened student of relationships. The sad reality is that everyone places importance on looks, which fade with time, instead of the brain, which remains.

The real reason for discussing the working of the brain at this stage is not simply because of the importance of a functioning brain and a good emotional system to a relationship, but for something more profound. The fact is that these systems operate largely independently and when one operates the other two tend to shut down. In other words, you cannot be in the cortex and limbic systems at the same time. If you are in crocodile brain mode, then nothing else exists in that moment.

In a more basic sense, all human behaviour can be reduced to the fact that we can only think, feel or act. You cannot fully think and feel at the same time. The more you feel the less you think. When you date you are predominantly feeling, so the rational part of your brain is disabled (similar to simmering on the back of the stove). The emotions of love and lust lower your ability to think.

Love and lust are very powerful emotions of attraction. Your limbic system is in overdrive when you feel one of these attraction emotions. If you think about your first crush you will remember intense feelings, even for someone who didn't know you existed. We know that there are many different types of love. Two important ones are romantic love and companionship love. Romantic love in its full form lasts from 3 to 12 months. A small percentage of romantic love remains over the years, but usually the initial intensity wears off. Lasting relationships are based on companionship love, which is a warm and familiar feeling of closeness, not dramatic urges. Romeo and Juliette are the archetypal example of romantic love, ending with a tragic disaster. There was no evidence of effective frontal lobes exhibited in their behaviour.

The reason serial monogamy is so common is that Hollywood would have us believe that romantic love is what everyone seeks. Movies typically end with people falling in love. The movies should actually finish 10 years later after the couple has worked through the reality of building a lasting friendship. As a result, people seek one relationship after another trying to rekindle those feelings of romantic love.

Ironically, it is during this period of romantic love that you need the thinking brain the most – to assess the situation while you enjoy those loving feelings. Unfortunately, without the override, the off switch has been activated and you are now at the mercy of an emotionally charged and hormone-filled brain. This is not a safe place to be as the cognitive information which gives you warnings is being overridden. In other words, even if you know what the flashing neon warning lights are saying, you will not pay attention to them. Unless you put in place a conscious override to examine your relationships at a thinking level, it might be too late by the time the passionate attraction has worn off. You might have connected to the wrong type of person. Everything I share with you in this book requires you to apply knowledge early and efficiently, however, you need to realise that when you require your thinking brain the most, you are least able to access it because of the way the brain works.

Paradoxically, it seems that our basic biology wants us to attract and bond before we analyse and relate. Breeding is a higher order need than many other needs in life. In fact, the human species might be extinct by now if we analysed first rather than mated. Survival of the species requires reproduction before other higher order needs (such as feeling happy with our breeding partner). It is for this reason that people often have sex after funerals. A funeral might be depressing, but the fear of extinction drives the desire to reproduce. The drive to survive allows us to be emotional rather than rational beings for key biological functions, including reproduction.

If a prospective partner does not activate the emotional side of your brain, then they are probably not worth the effort. Therefore, the more your emotions are activated the better a person will be for you emotionally, but those emotions create a fog in your mind making it harder to properly assess that person. The key is that the emotional activation might be a healthy love attraction or some deeper attraction which could turn out to be pathological. You must apply the love finder tools to achieve something more than just a primitive desire to mate. You need to control your brain to obtain lasting happiness in your relationship. The cortex rules – okay?

Love Finder Tools:

- If your prospective partner does not activate your emotional mind, then what is the point of pursuing the relationship? Emotional reactions are good indicators that there is something about this person which activates you. The task is to determine if it is a healthy activation. Monitoring your reactions and knowing yourself are key tools.

- Your emotional brain will override your logical brain when emotions run high. You must activate the deliberate logical analysis to make an informed choice. Choose the cortex and let it rule – okay?

What is Personality?

IN A RECENT ASSESSMENT, a woman said that she met her partner Peter while she was at university. She said that she was attracted to his free spirit and lack of desire to follow convention. When asked for an example, she explained that while she was in a tutorial class, she saw Peter through the classroom window sitting barefoot on the lawn in the sun, talking to others rather than attending class. She saw a free spirit. I saw the flashing neon signs of a personality disorder.

Every day we hear expressions such as "she has a great personality", "that person has a difficult personality" and, increasingly in the media and online, "she has borderline personality disorder" (men can have it too but this is frequently attributed to women) or "he is narcissistic" (women can also be narcissistic, but this is more frequently applied to men). Therefore, we need to unpack what all this means.

Psychology defines personality in rather bland and unexciting ways, such as a characteristic and consistent way in which people relate to the world. While not very exciting, such definitions are very helpful. If something is not consistent, we could never predict it. The literature includes a lot of arguments around personality and disorders, but those arguments are not helpful here. We need to understand that people will typically do the same thing each time they are in the same situation. For example, if you tend to be shy when meeting a new person, then shyness might be considered a personality trait. We know, however, that shyness is often selective – you could be shy in a large group but fine in a small group. In this way there are aspects of personality which are not predictable as a personality trait alone. It means that people have some characteristics unique to them and many characteristics which are more general.

Returning to the story of the woman and her partner Peter. What is wrong with sitting barefoot in the sun or being a "free spirit"? For me, the neon warning lights are that Peter does not follow conventions, he is not working when he is supposed to, and what he is doing is all about him. As the story unfolded, the woman spoke of Peter not holding down jobs, not finishing things, and making hundreds of promises but not being able to keep them. Worse still, she explained that he justified what he did and never took responsibility. She felt he was more like a child than a partner. Personality is consistent and therefore his issues were predictable.

As another example: your boss steals your ideas and presents them as his own. When you confront him, you experience an adult raging at you like a 4-year-old having a tantrum, so you back down. Here you see a pattern of behaviour which is dysfunctional. Everyone avoids this person who justifies his position because he is "special". This where psychologists start to define personality disorder. Personality traits become signs of personality disorder when the person keeps engaging in behaviour which is dysfunctional and, despite the negative consequences, they keep repeating the same behaviour by justifying and rationalising what they are doing.

For the armchair psychologists among you, formally diagnosing a personality disorder is a complex and difficult process.

Analysing a person's patterns of behaviour takes time and expertise, including interviews with others who know the person. The person with a personality disorder can also act normally for short periods of time or when they need to. It is only in the crucible of stress that the full disorder is readily apparent. That crucible of stress can be ignited by rejection, pressure, and wounding in particular. What better place to experience all of these than in a relationship? At work, it may not be as evident, however, work is still an area where relationships exist so the same problems will emerge (but not as obviously as in the home).

When it comes to personality, there is a range of factors which shape how someone functions in the world. As discussed in the previous chapter, brain factors impact upon how we relate to one another and whether we are overly emotionally aroused or, at times, under-aroused. This alone is not enough to account for personality but is one of the building blocks to explain why some people will continue to repeat the same patterns of behaving in a dysfunctional way. If the brain switches on, then it will overreact each time. Later in the book I examine why childhood and attachment are relevant to personality traits. For the moment, be aware that both biological and environmental factors are relevant to the development of personality traits.

We need to understand normal personality before discussing disorders. In my experience, I have never actually met a normal person, however, there are a lot of unique people who are very functional – and that is normal enough for me. The research shows that underneath general day-to-day traits there are five broad personality factors. Psychologists refer to this as the five-factor model of personality. These make up broad dimensions which are present in everybody to varying degrees. The point to note is that we all have these characteristics – it is just that some people have a higher level of certain characteristics. Everyone's uniqueness is shaped by how much is present and how the traits are packaged together.

The first of these five factors is called "openness". Some people are open to new experiences – they want to try many different or new activities and will tolerate new and original ideas. Other people tend to be closed to new experiences and often feel suspicious of the beliefs of others which might change their own status quo. People who tend not to be open prefer consistent routines and tend to value safety and predictability.

It is important to have some idea of whether you tend to be a fairly open or a closed individual, as this will impact upon your ability to relate to your partner. It does not really matter on which end of the spectrum you sit, but this is a dimension where similarity becomes important. That is, it is very helpful if both partners have similar levels of adventurousness or need for safety.

The second factor is "conscientiousness". The conscientious person is one who is aware of their behaviour and the consequences of that behaviour. They tend to be well-organised, tidy, good at timekeeping, and they tend to be more goal orientated. They are likely to be socially responsible and have a clear sense of guilt when things are not right (according to social norms). Unconscientious people tend to be more impulsive and make last-minute decisions. This can be quite fun in the moment but, in terms of making a long-term relationship work, the conscientious person is going to be more reliable and sensible (and these are better long-term variables on which to build a relationship). Conscientiousness traits result from strong frontal lobes and secure attachment.

"Extroversion" and "introversion" are well-known characteristics. These words feature in everyday life. Historically it was thought that there was a strong biological component. That is, an extrovert was thought to be somebody who had a sluggish nervous system and sought excitement through adventure, social behaviour and outgoing activities to stimulate an arousal in which to feel normal. On the other hand, the introvert was someone who had a very sensitive nervous system and, as a result, tended to feel shy around others, preferred more solitary activities, was less social and worked best on their own or in smaller groups, preferably with familiar people.

This biological concept of extroversion has lost vogue in psychology but is still a helpful concept. In this part, we are talking about how the emotional brain impacts upon how we react to the world (and that makes sense). Whether or not there are other causes to the development of these characteristics (as is being debated in psychology), the traits are firmly entrenched in the world of personality.

It is a very common relationship pattern when someone who tends to be an introvert is drawn to, and goes out with, someone who is an extrovert. This relationship brings excitement into an introvert's life and allows them to push past the isolation they have experienced. In the short to medium-term this is fun. However, as the relationship progresses in the longer term, this once very positive factor becomes the source of resentment. The introvert now complains because their extrovert partner wants to go out all the time, and the extrovert complains because the introvert is trying to limit social activity. This is a relationship variable which ideally should be matched between partners. In saying this, there is not a better type of personality to match with as it depends on what you are like. Two introverts together at home watching a science documentary may be in heaven; while the same introvert going with an extravert to a night club to hear loud dance music might feel that they are in psychological hell.

"Agreeableness" refers to the degree of cooperativeness within which people operate. Someone with high agreeableness tends to be considered likeable by their peers and colleagues, is more altruistic and helps others in time of need. They tend to dislike conflict and seek to pacify problems. People who are disagreeable tend to be less concerned with pleasing people, are more suspicious about other people's motives, and are less charitable. It should be noted that although some personalities do not change, people tend to become more agreeable with time.

You probably do not need me to point out just how significant this variable is when it comes to being happy in a relationship. Nobody likes to date a grump. In the extreme form, a disagreeable person might be paranoid about other people in negative and extreme ways. On your dating checklist, ensure that you tick the agreeableness box before your second or third dates.

"Neuroticism" is a personality trait which refers to emotional stability. People who tend to be emotionally stable are low on neuroticism. They tend to be fairly well grounded. Somebody who is high on neuroticism tends to be emotionally unstable – they are worriers and are fearful and anxious. They tend to exaggerate the size of their problems and dwell on the negative aspects of life. You know that your partner is high on neuroticism when, for example, on a windy night they are in the garden looking to see if someone is there (even though you know it was just the wind), if they accuse you of chewing your food too loudly, or if they scream loudly when a small fright occurs. Someone who is neurotic tends to be highly strung and variable.

Studies have shown that people in relationships are less happy when their partner scores high on neuroticism. Furthermore, people who are emotionally unstable are a lot harder work for their partner, life is a lot less predictable, and periods of joy are less frequent. In older psychology parlance we used to describe people as neurotic. This term is no longer in vogue, but it is still appropriate in some cases.

It is important to know that someone particularly high on the neuroticism trait will function differently to normal people. Whereas most people function by seeking pleasure, these people often try to avoid emotional pain. They have elaborate behaviours to lower their anxiety. The most significant of these behaviours is control. When control is high, anxiety is lowered. If someone is neurotic, they need to be in control to make life less painful.

If your partner is high on the neurotic scale, they will require you to do things on their terms. It is very difficult to be in a relationship with someone who must have everything done their way. When coming out of a relationship with someone who has required such control, there is a sense of freedom and relief because you will no longer feel like you are constantly walking on eggshells. That kind of relationship is a very difficult place from which to operate. People in these relationships are often dependent or needy themselves – trying to fix problems gives them a purpose in life.

The starting point for choosing a good partner is to consider the five factors of personality discussed above. Where it escalates to another level is when these factors sometimes combine in a way which results in dysfunction. When the Diagnostic & Statistical Manual (DSM-V) – the bible of psychiatric diagnosis – was revised, an eminent group of personality theorists realised that the previous theory of personality disorder did not work very well. They proposed that personality disorder is really the extremes of these five factors, and different combinations of these factors results in different profiles of how people will present. The point is essentially that while all of us have these factors, some of the factors have negative implications for successful and happy relationships. It is important to look for the signs of these conditions in long-term relationships.

The triad of traits to avoid are high neuroticism, a lack of conscientiousness and a lack of agreeableness. These traits are the ones that make relationships extremely difficult in the long run. They are serious negative indicators which can impact upon the success of a relationship. People who are unstable, unreliable or negative are high maintenance and will eventually sap your energy and personality. The biggest problem is that you will spend your time trying to appease the person with these traits rather than being yourself.

Love Finder Tools:

- Each of the five personality factors or traits are important considerations for successful relationships. Are you and your partner similar on the traits of openness and introversion / extraversion? Similarity in these traits will make the relationship easier and more successful. Check the match between you and your partner.

- Is there evidence of higher levels of neuroticism, a lack of conscientiousness or a lack of agreeableness? These are negative indicators which can impact upon the success of a relationship. People who are unstable, unreliable or negative will be hard work, demanding and destructive. Do not discount these factors when in the early stages of love.

Personality Disorders

IN THE RUINS OF A relationship of ten years, a woman discovered that her partner had had a methamphetamine addiction for ten years. She had no idea that he had made hundreds of calls to prostitutes and gambled hundreds of thousands of dollars. There were rumours of affairs. He had forged documents and borrowed massive amounts of money. She did not have a clue about the extent of his double life because he was always able to explain things. When meeting others he was amazingly smooth, and he made others feel special. He could not see that he had done anything wrong. Welcome to the aftermath of a personality disorder with a drug problem.

Barely a Family Court referral crosses my desk without allegations that one person is narcissistic or psychopathic, or that the other is borderline or histrionic. Sometimes these are correct diagnoses because the people suffering these conditions often end up in court. It is common sense to realise that there has to be something that prevents people from being reasonable and settling the matter themselves. At times, the person who has the disorder is projecting – accusing their partner of what they themselves have said or done – so that the words are actually applied in the opposite. This is because someone might feel that if their partner was not meeting their needs, the partner must be the one with the problem. In other words, sometimes it is the accuser who is the real culprit as they find that a strong offence is the best form of defence.

One of the more interesting social psychology processes is what psychologists call retrospective attribution. This means that when viewed in hindsight the relationship must have been really bad or the couple would not have separated. For example, a religious person marries until death us do part. If the couple separates, the relationship must have been terrible in order to justify the breaking up of the marriage. Therefore, some people project onto their partner the traits of a personality disorder as a way of making sense of what has happened.

Finally, personality disorder is frequently being diagnosed on the basis of popular media's perceptions applied to normal traits. Diagnosis by "Dr Google" is a risky and unreliable business causing confusion. It is important to know that there are many paths to personality disorder and only some of them are true.

Personality disorder is frequently discussed in the popular media, which is probably why you have picked up this book in the first place. The DSM-V (mentioned earlier) identifies into ten broad groups people who are extremely dysfunctional in terms of personality (but who are not suffering from a particular mental illness even though personality disorder is itself sometimes classed as a mental illness). There are three clusters. Cluster A relates to odd, bizarre and eccentric personality types (paranoid, schizoid and schizotypal). Cluster B covers the dramatic and erratic personality types (including anti-social, borderline, histrionic and narcissistic personalities). Cluster C refers to the anxious and fearful personality types (avoidant, dependent and obsessive-compulsive). The problem with these is that, while they sound good in theory, the different types tend to blur into one another with many overlapping characteristics. For those of you interested in correct diagnosis, if a person has the traits of several types of disorder it is called Personality Disorder Not Otherwise Specified (NOS). While NOS is technically the most common type of personality disorder, it tells us nothing of what the person is like.

Due to the problem of NOS and other technical issues, the DSM-V revision committee wanted to revert to mixes of the extremes of the five factors (rather than keeping the separate types). It is an intrinsically more appealing position to see personality as an extension of normal 5-factor traits which become intense and rigid, than a disease model. That way, rather than having or not having a disorder, there can be a little bit of disorder. Take for example narcissism. A very narcissistic person has excessive and unreasonable views of their own successfulness, making grand plans which fail. Almost every successful person in life needs to believe in themselves despite any failures. When does the latter healthy degree of narcissism cross the line from being good for success into the destructive path of repeated failures? There is no clear line.

Notwithstanding the issues outlined above, the ten separate types of personality characteristics in Clusters A, B and C do provide a lot of information about how people function in relationships. While having a relationship with someone with any type of personality disorder is going to be difficult, the ones which generate drama and the greatest set of issues are the Cluster B personality types. Remember that the primary characteristics of this group are the dramatic and erratic patterns of behaviour. The Cluster B personality types will be discussed in the next paragraphs.

The person with an anti-social personality disorder is essentially the psychopath. The forensic psychologist in me needs to highlight that all psychopaths have antisocial personality disorders, but not all antisocial personality disorders are psychopaths. In other words, you can be a rule breaker, get into trouble with the police, but not necessarily lack empathy or use people for your personal pleasure. I should also briefly add that the term psychopath has been misapplied in the popular media and includes terms such as "corporate psychopath" and "sharks in suits". While there are plenty of self-centred businesspeople with a callous disregard for others, they are not necessarily psychopaths. More likely they are narcissistic. I will leave the professionals to argue about the definition. What you need is more of an understanding of the personality type.

Those people who have an anti-social personality disorder are characterised by a callous disregard for the feelings of others. By this I mean that they tend to feel that other people exist to serve them, and they get upset and become difficult when people do not support what they want. Perhaps one of the most interesting aspects (from a dating point of view) is that the research tends to suggest that these types of people tend to have a greater number of partners, dates and relationships than other people. A common characteristic of this type of person is that superficially they appear charming, so people are drawn into a relationship with them. The relationships, however, quickly become fiery and turbulent and, as a result, are short-lived. Similarly, as these people are self-centred, they are more likely to have affairs while in a relationship.

When crossed, these people are inclined to hurt the ones with whom they have had a relationship because they do not care about feelings. They will use whatever means they can to get their needs met, even it means hurting and using the people they are close to. One of the more disturbing aspects of this personality type is that they often work from the position of "I don't get mad, I get even". They might at times rage to get what they want but will use violence and other forms of payback in strategic ways.

For example, during a marriage counselling session with me a couple spoke about a recent argument. The husband had woken up in the morning and wanted sex, but the wife said no. They went to church and he spent three hours ruminating about how he would cause an argument on the way home about something she had done – he planned to jump out of the car so that she would have to drive back and pick him up. She would feel guilty and then he would have sex. The plan worked like clockwork and he got his sex. However, the cost of it was that his wife felt humiliated and manipulated to the point that she wanted to leave the marriage. Marriage counselling for this couple was dangerous and could not continue because he would present nicely in the session but then punish her in the car on the way home for the things she had said which he felt defamed his character.

A second group in the Cluster B personalities is the borderline personality disorder. These people are frequently discussed in the press and on websites. This is often viewed as a disorder in women, but men can also be diagnosed with the condition. There is also a debate around complex trauma and borderline personality disorder, meaning that a longstanding trauma might be affecting patterns of behaviour rather than it being an actual disorder of personality. Many of the people who have this diagnosis come from terribly abusive childhoods and their reactions are symptoms of trauma. For our purposes, if the behaviour is characteristic and enduring, the cause matters less than how that person reacts. The biggest implication for the different causes is the way in which the disorder is treated to achieve recovery.

People with this disorder tend to feel empty, lack a sense of self, and have strong fears of abandonment. If a person does not have a strong sense of self it makes them very changeable and they must rely on others to feel normal. Because these people are so needy, they tend to draw others in to support them. They have also learned how to tell stories in a way which hooks people in to rescue them. When in a relationship, these people are like bottomless pits and no amount of assistance is going to fill the hole. When someone tries to leave them, the person with this condition experiences a massive sense of abandonment and may act out with suicidal threats or threats of self-harm, and might become extreme in their behaviour to either try to stop the person leaving or to regulate their own overwhelming emotions. However, when it suits them, they can turn on the helplessness. For example, one moment they are completely out of control, but that then switches off when a third party arrives. A complicating factor is that these people can be quite seductive in manner and appearance resulting in the relationship progressing extremely quickly after the initial meeting.

Similar to the anti-social personality disorder, the person with borderline personality disorder has several ways of drawing people in. First by being needy, which attracts rescuers, and second by being seductive and charming. The intensity of the emotions in the initial stages of a relationship with someone with borderline personality disorder can be mind-blowingly intense but almost always short-lived. There are plenty of people who are drawn in by either of these personalities. The full intensity of the underlying drama is not evident until later.

The next of the Cluster B personalities is the histrionic personality disorder. The word "histrionic" derives from the Latin "histrionicus", meaning pertaining to the actor. The word hysterical is another derivative. You can see where this going. These people survive by attracting attention and seeking the approval of others, and they lack a sense of worth. As a result, they become quite dramatic. When we refer to someone as a "drama queen", it is a reference to their histrionic pattern of behaviour. A person like this can place themselves at risk of accident and exploitation, can be overly charming, inappropriately seductive, and their ability to deal with people tends to be quite superficial.

The dynamics can be a vicious circle – the more that person is rejected, the more histrionic they become and the more they act out. Hence the rejection at the end of the relationship will lead to some of the most extreme acting out behaviour. At times this overlaps with the patterns of behaviour of the borderline personality disorder. For example, both groups may threaten suicide to try to bring their partner back. The difference is subtle. The histrionic person is largely not suicidal but uses drama to manipulate, whereas the borderline type commonly uses the threat of self-harm to try to regulate emotions.

The last group in Cluster B are the narcissistic personality disorders. Among the key diagnostic characteristics of this condition are extreme feelings of self-importance, a sense of entitlement, and a need to be admired and respected. This person is envious of others and expects others to be envious of them. There is a lack of sincere empathy and they readily exploit others to achieve their aims. When they do not get their needs met, they can fly into a rage (akin to that of a 4-year-old having a tantrum – except that they are an adult). If somebody upsets them, this person will often fly into a narcissistic rage and will direct their anger at, and seek revenge against, the person who upset them.

From a relationship point of view, in the short-term the narcissistic personality seems to be confident and self-assured, very successful, and is attractive because of their confidence. They will be exceptionally generous in the early stages. They will share plenty of stories about grand schemes and past successes. It may be possible to miss the fact that the stories are always about them. They form relationships because the person seems to be successful and in control. Most mature people want a relationship with someone who is successful. It is only as time passes that the self-centredness of the personality becomes evident to all those around them. While you are feeding their ego, they will be generous and happy. It is only when they experience the word "no" that the rage emerges. As explained earlier, there is a bit of narcissism in everyone but larger amounts in successful people. To be able to spot at an early stage those with excessively high levels of narcissism can be quite tricky even for a highly trained professional tasked with identifying the patterns. The man described at the start of the chapter (the methylamphetamine addict who had been in a relationship for ten years) was an "entrepreneur" but never contributed to the family income. Within six months of separation, and while unemployed, he bought his new partner a $40k wedding ring.

While the above exemplars represent some of the clearest types of personality disorders in people who are difficult to live with, it is important to realise that relationships are made more difficult by things other than personality disorders. Personality traits can be destructive even if they do not necessarily meet the full-blown criteria of a personality disorder. Traits including a lack of empathy, heightened drama, neediness and other associated actions are not foundations for a loving relationship.

A common element of these four Cluster B personality types is that a person can present well for short periods of time and so they have an enhanced capacity to present exceptionally well in the initial stages of a relationship. This might include chameleon-like qualities such as appearing to be the person you want, being charming and seductive, or being able to trigger your desire to protect and help. Unfortunately, it is all an illusion. The smoke screen fades, and the real personality emerges over time. I will explain later that, because the initial smoke screen image felt so good, a partner will stay hoping that the real person will return, and that they will not be left with the nasty person they are currently with. Unfortunately, the current person is the real one, not the initial illusion.

As stated earlier, diagnosing a personality disorder is quite difficult because a person can present very well in the short-term. I remember saying in court that a person had a personality disorder, and the judge responded that he did not care about labels. He explained that he cared about how the person's behaviour impacted the children. Therefore, the key love finder tool from this section is that you do not need to care about whether you can diagnose what your partner has, rather it is how their pattern of behaviour impacts your relationship. There is no need for a diagnosis if there are strong elements of each of the above areas of personality disfunction.

Some people might tell you that they have been diagnosed with the above conditions. You do not have to stay with them and prove them right. If they think they fit the pattern (even if it is only according to Google) then be afraid, very afraid.

Love Finder Tools:

- All the personality disorders have the ability to present in a way that is especially attractive in the initial stages of a relationship. In fact, a person might present better than normal. If a person seems too good to be true, then you are probably right. It takes time to see a person's true nature.

- The key to recognising personality problems is that it is essentially all about that person and, while they get their way, the relationship will feel great. It is only when you want to establish boundaries or say "no" that the drama will become evident.

- Look at behaviour and not the internet. Diagnosis is not as important as recognising patterns of behaviour.

The Best Predictor of Future Behaviour is Past Behaviour

WHEN I WAS A PSYCHOLOGY student at university in my early twenties, I dated another student. To respect the person, I will call her Verity and change some general details but keep the essence of the story true to the situation. Verity was quite an attractive lady. She had modelled and had a portfolio of attractive modelling pictures (with the benefit of my years of training, I now know I should have been alert to the warning signs when Verity showed me these photos early on). When she was with me, she was lovely – warm, affectionate and loving. I dated Verity for approximately four months. One of the issues I found considerably frustrating was that she had very little real time for me. She would make a time to catch up or to go on a date but would cancel at the last minute or only come for half an hour. While her words were loving and supportive, her actions did not match up.

I never knew what she was doing to keep her so busy the rest of the time. She would tell elaborate stories, which were plausible but also suggestive of a chaotic life. There was always an explanation for her actions, although over time the reasons seemed less plausible. It got to the point that I wondered whether she had somebody else in her life. Out of frustration (because of never being able to catch up with her) I gave up on her and moved on to a new relationship when a better opportunity presented itself.

Interestingly, many years later when conducting a search of Psychology Registration Board complaints against psychologists, I discovered that Verity had been successfully prosecuted by the Board for having an inappropriate relationship with clients. This included having two people who thought they were engaged to her at the same time. I am positive that is what had happened with me – that is, that she had at least one other boyfriend in addition to me. Her behaviour had not changed over the years.

With the benefit of hindsight, I realised that there were some small indicators of her behaviour which should have told me that she was a risky partner. Rather than lasting four months, I probably should have ended the relationship after the first few rejections. However, like all people in the dating scene, my own insecurities at that time kept me coming back for more. I believed her stories because I took them on face value. If only I had the skill set of tools as a young adult that I have now!

This also demonstrates that her early behaviour was consistent over time, leading to her professional demise. Her life was full of repeated patterns of seeing multiple partners and, I have no doubt, she told them stories to make them believe that they were the only ones in her life. Herein lies one of the important aspects of psychology. Psychology can only predict behaviour because that behaviour is able to be predicted. The first rule of psychology is that the best predictor of future behaviour is past behaviour (unless there is an intervening variable).

This rule applies to many areas of psychology, not just dating. As a predictor of violence, sex offending or suicide, past actions are good indicators of future risk. In the case of family violence, if in the early years of a relationship someone slaps your face during an argument, that behaviour might be justified with several excuses. However, unless that person attends anger management counselling or personal therapy, that behaviour will be repeated in the future. Past behaviour is quite predictive of what will happen in the future. There is also a reasonable possibility in the case of face slapping that the level of reaction will increase in time thus becoming riskier and more dangerous, irrespective of how sorry they say they are about it.

It has been said the we are creatures of habit. This is indeed the essence of behavioural prediction from past behaviour. If you are a creature of habit you will generally respond in a consistent fashion. From a love finder point of view, this means that the more you can learn about someone's past behaviour the better you can predict the future. Another lady I dated at university (I'll call her Kathy) said that she had been in about 20 previous relationships, with none of them lasting more than three to six months. Kathy used to say that she did not do commitment. You can guess what happened. I was number 21 on the way to number 22. Kathy said that we had set a record for her because we had dated for nearly eight months. In my opinion, the longer period probably said more about me than Kathy in that dynamic.

At least Kathy knew what she was doing and had told me up front. I had a choice. I know that many people might be up front saying that "I don't do commitment", "I can't do monogamy" or "I don't want kids". People, however, don't listen to the words or look at the past. They live in hope, fanned by the flames of love from the emotional brain, and therefore expect that people will change. They are surprised when each of the above statements hold true.

Recently I asked someone what they knew about their former partner's past. They said, "I was not interested so I didn't ask". That is telling on two counts. First, they did not have an opportunity to apply the rule of how the past impacts the future. Second, it suggests a lack of empathy which in turn might suggest personality disorder traits. In my opinion, discussing a potential partner's past is one of the most useful things you can do.

On the same theme of past predicting future, a later chapter discusses disclosure and intimacy and will examine other aspects of sharing information from the past. That chapter will help you to determine whether you are getting either too much or not enough information. You need to understand that this knowledge is essential for both finding someone who is suitable and for avoiding those who are not.

A quirky aspect of human nature is the way in which we like to self-protect. There is a psychological process called the fundamental attribution error. In short, on average we will take personal credit for our successes but blame the environment or external situations for our failures. It is pretty neat how this can protect us. If something is my fault, I have to deal with the sense of inadequacy and failure, and I have to change. It is so much easier to blame another person or something external, because then it is not my fault and I do not need to change. When you ask someone about their past, understand that the person is likely to self-protect. It is common to be told that a person's last relationship broke up because of their partner – "it was not my fault"!

These self-deceptions are what psychologists call a cognitive bias. We all have a distorted view of both the past and reality. Therefore, when trying to understand someone's past you need to know that they will do this, and you have to see through it. The more extreme the stories, especially the more another person is blamed (rather than recognising their own actions), the more critical you should be – you might be their new ex-partner. The worst mistake you can make is to unquestioningly believe the stories about an ex-partner. Significantly, if you can access a third-party version (such as meeting the ex-partner yourself, looking at the communications between them, or talking to family members), the more you will be able to override this bias.

A friend's mother used to say that in every relationship problem there were three parts – what you did, what they did, and the situation. While there are many situations which are not comprised of equal parts, there is always some of each. The more evidence you uncover from those past stories that the person accepted some of the responsibility, the more psychologically mature that person is likely to be.

Recently I spoke to a man who said that his affair with another woman broke up the marriage. A good start – he seemed to take responsibility. He then went on to tell me that he and his wife had not had sex for eight months and therefore it was all his wife's fault. When I queried him further, the eight months was when his wife was pregnant with a high risk pregnancy. Applying the best predictor rule, as soon as the relationship encountered a problem, he justified getting his needs met elsewhere.

I stated that the best predictor of future behaviour is past behaviour unless there is an intervening variable. An intervening variable is something which changes a person. To revisit a previous example, if someone has a history of domestic violence there is no reason to expect it not to happen again unless they have done something about it. For example, they may have gone to counselling, undertaken anger management, or treated their trauma. However, it is the attitude change, not the course they complete, which is the intervening variable. To explain further, if your partner claims they have completed an anger management course but when they talk about their past you might still hear that it was all their ex's fault for triggering their anger. As such, they have not received good therapy and the behaviour is likely to happen again. The sinister implication is that when you act in a similar way to an ex-partner, it will be you who experiences the negative behaviour next (unless the person really has changed).

While on the topic of change, people do learn from life experiences, they mature with age, and gain benefit from counselling. However, there needs to be evidence of change before you can accept that the change is real. There is a difference between counselling and therapy. Talking about your problems may make you feel happy, but it does not necessarily change you. Therapy is about changing underlying patterns of thinking and acting. Therefore, identifying intervening variables is helpful, but you need to see the fruits of the change.

In my professional capacity, I once assessed a separated mother of two children who came from a wealthy background. She had a drinking problem. With an unacceptably high blood alcohol reading and her kids in the car, she had a car accident. The father, who wanted majority care and was refusing to return the children, did not want her driving the car with the children in it. When I saw the mother, she was undergoing personal therapy and had completed three sessions of alcohol counselling. She told me that she only drank because her ex-husband made her feel stressed, but that she was now cured of her drinking problem. I refused to recommend the return of the children to majority care because she was not taking responsibility for her actions and nothing had changed. Nine months later, the 5-year-old child had to call an ambulance when she found her mother unconscious and in a pool of vomit on the lounge room floor. The mother had been drinking. After this experience the mother underwent a 12-month residential alcohol course. Subsequently she was able to own her part in the situation and believed the Alcoholics Anonymous creed that "you are only one drink away from being an alcoholic". She understood that it was her choice, not the stress from someone else, making her drink. This was suggestive of real change.

As you can see, the intervening variable is important for understanding behaviour change. It is not just what the person has done, but whether you can see evidence of the manifestation of real change. It is important to remember that behaviour comprises both actions and thoughts. Either of these are important. Past behaviour shows how a person really acted, but thoughts enable you to determine why they are acting in the way they do.

One factor with respect to past behaviour being predictive (and which I find exciting), is that generally the more disturbed a person is the more likely they are to become a creature of habit. One of the defining characteristics of personality disorder is that dysfunctional patterns are repeated without change. The behaviour operates like a script to the same, usually disastrous, outcome.

There are several tests that will be discussed in more detail in future chapters. Of these, I should have applied what is called the 90% rule to Verity and given her the "No-test". If I had done that, I am sure that I would have been much more certain that I was in a relationship that was not going to lead to love, but to disaster and heartbreak. The reason that these tests work is that behaviour is consistent. The principle that the best predictor of future behaviour is past behaviour is one of the corner stones of making a good assessment.

One of my supervisors stated that one past marriage = made a mistake; two past marriages = has trouble learning from the mistake; three past marriages = personality disordered because they do not learn from mistakes. (Here, "marriage" is used in the sense of a serious long-term committed relationship, irrespective of legal status.) The past relationship history of a prospective partner is a rich area of psychological information to explore. Three failed relationships of substance are warning signs in their own right.

With respect to past behaviour, I have focussed on identifying past bad behaviour as predictive. It is also important to realise that past good behaviour is also predictive. If your new partner has had only one previous relationship which lasted 10 years, then it is reasonable to hope they have the skills to make your relationship work. Look for evidence of good past behaviour as that will also be helpful.

Consequently, the love finder toolbox includes a study of past relationships. It is critical to understand the past to discover how that has shaped how a person has developed their personality and responded in past relationships.

Love Finder Tools:

- Your prospective partner's past is a like a mirror which will reflect, to some degree, what it will be like for you in the future, because the best predictor of future behaviour is past behaviour.

- The past predictor rule means that the more you can discover about your partner's past, the greater the chance to see what it will be like for you with that person.

- The fundamental attribution error means that we see ourselves as innocent parties and that someone else is responsible for problems that occur. When considering someone's self-reported past, consider that it might be distorted by this bias. If possible, obtain evidence from other sources.

- People can make mistakes and then change if they learn from those mistakes. However, you need to see evidence of real changes in attitudes and actions to be sure that the future will be different.

Before You Buy a Horse, Check Out the Stable

CONSIDER THE FOLLOWING EXAMPLE. A 4-year-old child runs down a hallway, trips on the edge of the carpet, falls to the ground and gets carpet burns to both knees. He is highly distressed. In one scenario, his mother runs to him, picks him up, pats him down and says "There, there dear, this will get better." In another scenario, his mother shouts at him saying "You're stupid. How many times have I told you not to run in the house?" or "You're clumsy, you should watch where you're going. Stop whingeing and don't come near me. It's your fault." The first scenario illustrates a parent with a healthy, balanced attitude. The second illustrates the opposite.

Flash forward two decades. That same child is now an adult and is in a relationship. He has a problem in that relationship. The child from the first scenario above, because of the experiences growing up, is able to resolve the problem in his current relationship by soothing emotions and understanding that the relationship will not end. The child from the second scenario, because of the poor experiences growing up, now feels inadequate and has no way of regulating the emotion within his current relationship and, as a result, could spiral into depression and anxiety or attack a partner who criticises.

This example describes a process called attachment, which refers to the way in which a child develops secure relationships with the people in their life and learns how to regulate their emotions. If the child's needs are met, that will build trust and stability. It is essential to realise that these early relationships shape how a person relates to everyone else throughout their life. If you cannot trust your mother or father to be emotionally supportive, how can you trust your partner?

The first scenario in which the parent soothes the hurt child is described as developing a stable pattern of attachment, whereas the second scenario is described as having an unstable pattern of attachment. These patterns are cumulative. When dealing with situations, every parent will make mistakes. For example, from time to time a very tired parent might snap at their child instead of nurturing them. However, if the parent realises what they have done and then apologises to the child, the child learns the skills to repair relationships. In fact, the parenting literature has long said that children should not have a perfect response from parents all the time but should have "good enough" responses sometimes. This does not mean that a child should receive mediocre parenting. Instead, they should have good parenting which sometimes experiences problems. The good enough parenting allows a child to build the skills to repair relationships. The child learns ways to fix problems.

These early patterns of attachment are part of what shapes personality disorders (which are also shaped by biological aspects and trauma). If a child usually receives a loving response, it is reasonable to expect that they will feel safe and secure. If a child sometimes receives a loving response and sometimes an angry response, they will feel confused and ambivalent. If the child receives no response, they will feel helpless, disconnected or rejected. Finally, if the child never receives a supportive response, they will retreat emotionally and feel bitter or angry.

Note that this is not intended to be a criticism of parents. It is simply an explanation of how the most important early relationships in life are the basis from which we are taught to manage emotions. If you do not receive the right experiences, you do not learn. It has been said that practice makes perfect but that is only partly true. Practice makes perfect only if errors are corrected. Practice within a dysfunctional family relationship will only teach someone how to act in a dysfunctional manner.

One of the best tests to determine whether you are going to be in a healthy or unhealthy relationship is to review the family history of your future partner. If someone says that they have come from a relatively stable background, the chances of them having a stable personality style is likely to be much higher than if they have come from a highly dysfunctional background. It should, however, be noted that people like to paint a positive picture of their history and life.

A rich source of background information can be obtained by visiting your partner's family, and this information can help fix the problem in the relationship. You will be able to see how the family members respond to one another. The way in which your partner treats their parents is often an indicator of how you will be treated. If you see your partner interacting with their family with respect and understanding, then it is likely that your partner will respect and understand you. However, if your partner is particularly critical (especially towards their parent of the opposite sex), then it is likely that you will experience similar criticism.

With respect to families, it is important to note that first, it is the breeding ground for either stable or unstable attachment capacities (which then shapes how personalities function) and second, it is the forum within which people learn implicitly. Our characters are shaped by the things we see, hear and experience when we are growing up.

It is said that that if a live frog is put into boiling water it will try to escape. However, if a frog is put into cold water, and the temperature is slowly increased, the frog will stay in the water until boiled. Apparently, frogs don't have receptors to detect changes in heat. I have never carried out this experiment, but it makes a lot of sense. Someone from a dysfunctional background might not realise how dysfunctional their background was. They have no way of knowing whether the water is hot or cold. As an observer, you can look at your partner's background independently to see how much dysfunction there was.

Differences between families will have a lot of influence on the way in which partners relate to one another. According to my wife, her mother was somewhat histrionic and, as a way of dealing with problems, would react with hurtful comments such as "they say that beauty is skin deep, but you don't even have beautiful skin". During her first big argument with a boyfriend, my wife reacted with similar catastrophic statements such as "I wish I had never met you". She said that the look of devastation on her boyfriend's face shocked her into realising how unusual and dysfunctional this style of communication could be. Fortunately for me, this was an intervening variable for my wife, and she realised that she needed to be different. By the time I met her, she was past this reactive pattern of interacting.

Differences between families can shape everything from expectations for birthdays, to child rearing practices and communication styles. We are shaped by our experiences and we therefore see our frame of reference as correct and other people's expectations as weird. The following personal example illustrates this point. I grew up in a family with three siblings. My parents never celebrated wedding anniversaries. When with a friend on his family's farm, his parents celebrated their twentieth anniversary. At the time I was utterly convinced that this was weird because my parents had never celebrated a wedding anniversary. A few years later I found out that my parents had both previously been divorced, I had six additional half siblings, and my brother was conceived out of marriage (which was considered shameful in the 1960s). It is no wonder that my parents did not celebrate anniversaries. It was a bitter pill to swallow when I realised that I was the one who held the weird views on celebrating wedding anniversaries. Darn that attribution error!

To further illustrate this point. One of my clients came from an Italian family. She said that when her family argued, they yelled and screamed and said things such as "I will never speak to you again" but then go out for coffee together the following day. She said that her husband came from an English background and his family never expressed their emotions. After twenty years of marriage, her view was that "he never got used to the Italian way" and his view was that "I had twenty years of walking on eggshells to stop her from being emotionally abusive". I think that they were both probably right because they had been shaped by very different experiences. Each saw their own behaviour as normal and that their partner had the problem. Therefore, differences can be real or imagined but will still have a huge impact over time.

Love Finder Tools:

- Families are the building blocks for the way in which people's capacity to interrelate is constructed. A family's background is rich in information about a person's experiences when growing up. People from stable families are much more likely to be stable partners. Look for stability factors.

- Visit the family and observe their interactions and how they treat one another. Families built on supportive styles of communication, where people treat each other with respect, ensures that you will have a good platform upon which to build a relationship.

- Cultural differences impact upon a person's ability to relate to others. Understand differences in family upbringing.

- Observe how your partner treats their parents, especially the parent with the same gender as you. The way in which girls treat their mothers and boys treat their fathers provides clues – that is, how your partner will relate to you and what they will expect from you.

"Aisle" Change Him

Many little girls grow up fantasizing about the perfect wedding, picturing themselves walking down the <u>aisle</u>, after they have <u>changed</u> into their white dress, meeting their future husband while the <u>hymn</u> plays. This is a pattern sometimes applied by people to their relationships. In simple terms, a meaning is extracted from the above image of a wedding, "Aisle – change – hymn", translating it to "I'll change him". With respect to women, many like to fix problems leading them to form relationships with people who are broken, believing they can make the necessary repairs. Other variations include taming the rebel, mothering the needy and comforting the hurting boy. This leads someone to stay in a relationship with problematic dynamics, such as, trying to fix a partner with alcohol or another addiction, or dealing with a partner behaving badly (hoping that they will change their ways).

The male equivalent of this is the white knight charging to the emotional rescue. A damsel in distress provides a man with meaning and purpose so that they can feel valuable. For men who like to fix things, having someone to fix also gives a man meaning and purpose. However, if they do fix someone, they lose their superior role as a saviour and, if they do not fix someone, they gradually become resentful of the unreciprocated effort they've expended.

The cracks in these belief systems should now be apparent to you. The sad truth is that it is a myth that a partner can be changed in significant ways. Broken people are very hard to fix and, if you enter a relationship trying to change your partner into the person you want them to be, you will become very disillusioned. The partner you select should not be viewed as a lump of clay to be moulded into the person you want, but a complete and stand-alone person who adds to your life.

John and Judy Gottman are two eminent researchers in the area of relationship dysfunction. The Gottmans, with decades of research on couple counselling, have developed a theory that relationships have two sets of problems – perpetual problems and fixable problems. Long-term research on marriage counselling shows that, in the majority of cases, relationship counselling does not work (with something like three-quarters of couples separating despite attending counselling). The Gottmans' research shows that 69% of problems are perpetual problems and about 31% are fixable problems (actual problems which can be solved). The perpetual problems do not go away – they are unsolvable even with psychological therapy.

Flowing from this research, the Gottmans' advice is to uncover someone's problems when you are dating them. The goal of dating is to find a person with an existing set of problems which you can live with, because you won't be able to change that person. The goal is not to find a mythical person free of problems. This, in my opinion, is essential advice for finding love. There is no such thing as a perfect person and, even if you did find them, I can guarantee they will still squeeze the toothpaste incorrectly. It is important to realise that you are trying to find a partner who will be good for you, not one who is perfect.

As a very experienced psychologist, I have given evidence in court about the efficacy of therapy. One of the things I state frequently is that people can change by degree, not by nature. This correlates neatly with the Gottmans' research which says that 69% of problems are perpetual. A couple can change 31% of their problems (that is, their actual or fixable problems) if they are willing to solve them, but the bulk of their problems remain (that is, they are perpetual problems).

There are two components to the set of problems you can live with. The first relates to you and the second relates to your partner. The component related to you concerns self-knowledge. How can you determine whether problems are going to be compatible unless you are clear about what you do and don't like? We know that our sense of self increases with age. Therefore, the earlier in life lasting relationships are formed, the greater the chance we do not know what we stand for. It supports an argument for dating and marriage later, rather than sooner, in life.

The following example provides a relevant illustration. I once worked in a prison for juveniles, and my boss was a great leader. He would attend meetings and in response to items raised would say "negotiable" or "not negotiable". If someone suggested changing the timetabling – no problem. If someone suggested changing the menu – no problem. If someone wanted to change a security procedure – no, not negotiable. For him, routines and food were conveniences, but prison security was essential. He would not compromise on security because it mattered to him. There are plenty of things which can change, but others which cannot because they really matter to you. Do you know what your non-negotiable issues are?

To illustrate further, at start of an interview with a client I asked him "what was it about Jenny that made you want to date her?" His response was "I was new in town and wanted female friendship". This was not a deep and meaningful assessment of what he wanted. Jenny was female and available. Mmmm … I wonder what the outcome was when they separated 4 years later? "We never had anything in common and I hate her". In my opinion this dating style is "lucky dip" dating – meeting a random person hoping that a relationship will work. This can be caused by several things including feeling insecure about dating, a lack of knowledge, desperation, self-esteem issues, or being predatory. The underlying issue is that the partner is not a match based on compatibility, but availability.

I can still remember a time in my late teens, when in a telephone counselling training group, I saw a very attractive lady that I liked. At times we chatted during the breaks in training, and on a lot of criteria she appeared to be like me. A second lady lived near me and on one occasion needed a lift home. As a 19-year-old from an all-boys high school, my relationship skills were impressive in their absence. I used the lucky dip dating style by dating the girl who needed the lift, not the one I actually liked. Ironically, the first lady with whom I chatted to during the breaks was devasted to find out I was dating the second lady. I persevered with the relationship with the second lady for nearly three years but ended up miserable. I was too proud to give up easily!

There is a cure for the lucky dip dating style. I recommend that you make a checklist of relationship factors which matter to you. If you have some idea of what you are looking for, you will improve your chances of finding it. Without a clear idea of the type of partner you are seeking, you are resorting to the lucky dip (receiving a random prize in the hope it is something you are looking for). Making lists and looking for evidence of these factors sounds rather mechanical and clinical when you want the romantic love portrayed in the movies. Hollywood love is just actors pretending, but what you read in this book is reality-based science. If you want to maximise your chances of finding love, the logical brain needs a framework to work within when the level of emotion is high.

Not only do you want a list of features to look for, you need to classify those features according to whether they are negotiable or non-negotiable. You can then let go of the features that do not matter and keep the rest. In my case, high on my list is someone who is intellectually my equal. I have one now and we have been together for 30 years. It is still exciting to discuss ideas with her, which then stimulates me. However, my very first relationship (the lucky dip woman described above) lasted just three years because she was not academically inclined. I now look back on this with regret because, towards the end, I treated her as if she was not my equal and that behaviour was destructive to both of us. I think it affected our self-esteem and had us behaving in ways which left us full of regret. Linda and I really did not have much in common other than the initial love. When the love faded, there was nothing left. Eventually she rode off into the sunset seeking something else. By doing so, she put both of us out of our misery.

When considering compatibility factors, do not get hung up on finding all factors. If you have a 20-item checklist and then reject someone with only 19 of those factors, you are missing the point. Your number of criteria is too high. Conversely, if you only tick one or two boxes, you are lucky dipping and will most likely run into problems.

The bottom-line is that you should discover which problems you can live with and establish compatible factors after you have a framework to find them. In the next chapter I discuss the façade and how that impacts relationships. For the moment, the tool to take from this chapter is to try and identify your partner's problems, because they are the problems which will be in the relationship (that is, don't just look at how wonderful the person is). Make sure that the problems your partner has are problems you can live with.

Love Finder Tools:

- If 69% of relationship issues are perpetual problems, then it is critical that you find a set of problems you can live with for the rest of your life.

- People can change but only by degree. Don't go into a relationship in the belief you can change someone into the person you want.

- Knowledge of who you are, and the things that are negotiable and non-negotiable, are critical to be able to see what problems you might live with.

- Make a checklist of factors which are important to you in a relationship and mentally tick them off. However, do not wait for perfection.

The Façade

SHORTLY AFTER MY MOTHER-IN-LAW DIED, my wife and I went on a five week holiday. Before we left, my father-in-law Jim was obviously recently widowed and unhappy. When we returned from holiday, he excitedly introduced us to his new girlfriend who he had met during our absence. I clearly remember sitting at the dining table observing their interactions.

My father-in-law's new girlfriend was from the United Kingdom. Jim, my father-in-law, said that he would really like to go to England to see the country she'd come from and to visit her family. At the same time, I was thinking about the occasion my mother-in-law had dragged him kicking and screaming on a trip to Singapore for five nights – Jim hated to travel. In fact, I had never seen any evidence that he had any desire to travel. On the other hand, Jim's girlfriend said that she would really like to go out in Jim's boat (Jim was a keen fisherman and had been building a fibreglass vessel). Looking at this pale-skinned English rose, I failed to see any evidence of an adventurous, outdoorsy-type person in her character.

Subsequently they got married. Jim never went to England. His wife went out on Jim's boat once, got terribly sick and then banned him from using the boat on the weekends because she wanted him to spend them with her. He was allowed to go out on the boat on weekdays, but that was very restrictive because the rest of the family were not available. This case highlights a very common scenario. People create a façade to give a positive impression. It is normal human behaviour and occurs in many areas of life (for example, job applicants have been found to have a high percentage of false information in their applications). Impression management is a fact of life.

In my opinion, a person who does not employ at least some impression management is likely to be pathological or autistic. If you do not care enough to dress up, look good and have your best outward presentation you are likely to be in "a take me as I am" position. That position is egocentric or narcissistic, or at least lacking in social tact. This is probably not a good position for a relationship either. Imagine future arguments, such as going to dinner when your partner does not care how they are dressed, or relatives visiting but your partner is not interested and doesn't engage with them. The issue lies in the degree to which this takes place.

A façade can exist in varying degrees. Real estate provides a good analogy. On one level when you sell your house it makes sense to do some painting and tidy up the gardens. It is still the same house, but it has been made as neat and tidy as possible. That is normal impression management. The alternative is when the house is made to look like something it is not. The house only exists on the outside and does not match what is behind the front walls – akin to an old western movie where façades were built to create the image of a western town (but nothing actually exists behind the façade). It makes sense that someone will dress themselves to look their best for a date. However, some people create an entirely false persona and adapt that to suit the situation. Their personality in the short-term is like jelly, changing to the shape of the vessel in which lies. Only later do you discover what they are really like. It can be tricky to see through the façade to find the real person. A third style is akin to a bank foreclosure. The bank sells the house "as is" to recoup their investment, providing poor returns. Nothing is done to it.

In the early stages of a relationship, it is very important to try and see through the façade. In the next chapter I will discuss the internet and how that enables the creation of an even better façade, however, for the purposes of this chapter it is important to recognise that people can create an image. A little image management is an appropriate social skill, but some people engage in false advertising which is very deceptive.

One of the purposes of dating someone over a longer period of time is to help see through the façade. In the short-term anyone can look good. As weeks move into months, and months into years, the ability and desire to keep up a façade is reduced. Cracks will show. In my opinion, with respect to high-end impression management, it takes the better part of three months for the cracks to begin to show. Within a year the signs are usually present. Unfortunately, it is a lot harder to disentangle from your partner after a year. In some cases, after a year people have made commitments, become financially entangled through a joint purchase, moved in together, and possibly fallen pregnant. These types of factors change the dynamics of the relationship and make it harder to separate.

In my work in the Family Court, I frequently see couples who separated because they realised that they were not compatible, only for them to discover shortly after separating that they were pregnant. They then decide to have another go at the marriage. This ends in failure, however, it can take a torturous five or ten years to realise that the marriage is not going to work (and that can cause a lot of damage).

High conflict personalities and the personality disorder types often look better than good in the short-term. A narcissistic personality type is truly charming. Borderline and histrionic types, when stable, appear particularly loving and attentive (even seductive and enticing). In the short-term, people with anti-social personality disorders are very good at manipulating people into believing what they want them to believe.

A search of the literature on personality disorder uncovers a term called "love bombing". It sums up very well what happens with some personality types, that is, they treat someone as if they are extremely special and will have them eating out of the palm of their hand. It is about control. They then withdraw the bombing. Their partner keeps expecting the former behaviour to return (after all, the person knows how to make someone feel like a princess or prince). The original behaviour does return, but only when it is needed, for example, to cover bad behaviour, after violence, when the victim tries to leave, or when relatives are present. It is a tool – not real love.

The following example illustrates the use of charming behaviour to perpetrate crimes against others. Ted Bundy was one of America's worst serial killers. He confessed to approximately 30 homicides between 1974 and 1978. The true number of victims is unknown and is possibly much higher than 30. Many of Ted Bundy's female victims regarded him as handsome and charismatic, traits that he would exploit to win their trust. Typically, he would approach his victims in public places including the university where he studied. He would feign an injury or disability and engage the victim to seek help. For example, he would wear a fake cast on his arm, drop some books and ask for help to take the books to his car. Once at the car, he would push the person inside, restrain them, and then take them to a secluded place where they would lose their life. The key point of this example is that, because of his charming nature, Ted Bundy's victims were completely unsuspecting. Bundy was not a love bomber as he was not dating his victims, however, he was "charming" and "charismatic".

Certain personalities go over the top at the start of the relationship by making their partner feel special. For example, repeated texts during day to ask how the partner is and what they are doing. In the early stages of a relationship this is labelled "caring". After a while this is actually controlling and, after separation, it is stalking. The person looking for love understands that in the early stages of dating people put on a façade (but not a complete princess scenario). In my opinion, if someone does not think about you and is not being especially nice or caring, then the relationship might not work either. The key is in the degree and whether the behaviour is encouraging and uplifting or controlling.

The literature on personality disorders also refers to the stages of a relationship, with love bombing as the opening strategy. The person will create an idealized relationship such that their partner believes everything is perfect. The partner feels adored. Once the hook is in, the antisocial personality type will, for example, start to run hot and cold. This behaviour creates doubts in the mind of the partner (or victim). The partner feels that they should try harder to please (as that is what they are being told to do). In the process the partner holds onto the hope of the previously good relationship returning. A person who is treated badly can become addicted to the positive feelings and reactions which come from time to time. Normally people do not tolerate bad behaviour but, in this case, hope keeps pulling them back. In this process, the partner becomes devalued. The person with the antisocial personality becomes bored with their partner, so they treat them with contempt (further lowering the poor victim's self-esteem). After a period of abuse, the partner loses their usefulness and they are discarded (if lucky) or the harm towards them continues (for being so useless). The abuser will not care anymore because of the contempt they hold towards their partner. While it does not make sense intuitively, on a practical level this is how psychopaths gain power. A dog is loyal to an owner who kicks it because it does not know it can leave. Nice people do not kick dogs.

The greater the degree of the façade, the greater the likelihood of disappointment once the relationship starts. This disappointment may be simple (such as not travelling overseas as promised) or can extend to drastic and violent outcomes. As stated earlier, the goal of dating is to get past the initial façade to uncover the perpetual problems (to see whether the person has a set of problems you can live with).

Ultimately, if someone seems too good to be true, they probably are. Your goal is to get past the "too good to be true" and find out what your partner's true character is. Ironically, the more problematic personality types have worked out that they need to load the charm at the beginning to win people over. I think that everyone is a sucker for special attention, hoping that it will continue. Vulnerable people fall for these charms more easily. Personal vulnerability comes in many forms, for example, from childhood dysfunction, adult trauma, poor parenting, previous bad relationships, and mental or emotional problems. It is important to note that being emotionally competent and mentally well will improve your chances of selecting a good partner and avoiding being a victim.

People believe façades. Plenty of people stay in very dysfunctional relationships because they hope for a return of the façade. In other words, the narcissistic charm, which was so seductive and gave you so much attention, was highly rewarding. Once established in the relationship you are treated like dirt, but part of you believes that underneath that rough exterior (which can include violence or verbal or mental abuse) that nice person still exists.

I am sorry to tell you that the opposite is probably the case – the nice person was the façade and what you are dealing with now is the real personality. There is an expression in statistics called regression to the mean. Essentially, outliers gradually drift to the average. In this case, extreme positive behaviour gradually drifts back to normal behaviour. You might think that if a person was able to put on that positive behaviour to start with, they should be able to do it again. It is true that they were capable of doing it, but they were only acting. Once an actor is out of role, you see the real person. In this case, what you eventually see is that person's real personality (and it might not be a pretty sight).

Love Finder Tools:

- Creating a façade is a normal part of dating in the initial stage. However, the greater the façade the less you will know what you are getting into. Time and collateral information are essential in breaking down the façade.

- "Love bombing" – being overly attentive and caring – should be analysed very carefully. If it is too good to be true, then trust your gut and check it out.

- Don't waste your life trying to change someone back to the nice caring person you initially dated. What you have now is likely to be the real person.

You Can Get Anything Online

TECHNOLOGY IS AN INTEGRAL PART of life. A recent study in America found that 77% of adults considered it "very important to have their smart phones with them at all times". Additionally, in 2018 the number of households with internet access ranged from 37% in Africa to 89% in the USA (with rapid growth occurring in all countries). Obviously, many things can be accessed online, including relationships. With the rapidly expanding availability of technology, and the increased breakdown of the village, people are turning to the internet for relationships.

A study by Michigan State University found that couples who started their relationships online were 28% more likely to experience the breakdown of their relationship in the first year than couples who started their relationships after meeting face-to-face. The people who started their relationships online were also nearly three times more likely to divorce. Despite these statistics, the rate at which people are establishing dates online is rapidly rising. In the 18 to 24 years age group, approximately 10% were dating online in 2013 and 27% in 2018. Even in the older age group of 55 to 64 years, the rates had increased from 6% to 12%

over a similar time period. These rates are therefore increasing rapidly and, in my opinion, are probably an underestimation of the real figures.

In our busy world, people shop online for all sorts of things. It therefore makes perfect sense that for online dating, whether for casual affairs or finding a permanent partner, the internet offers a myriad of ways of finding a partner. It is outside the scope of this book to provide advice on suitable websites. I would caution, however, that there is a significant problem with scamming via websites. News outlets provide many stories of people becoming conned into believing that the person they are dating is real (and then sending money to them and losing it as a result). It turns out that these people are not legitimate. A recent phenomenon, called "catfishing", relates to people who are duped into providing material which is then used against them. The "catfish" creates a false persona using existing images from that material. For example, there was the case of an unfortunate American soldier whose image was used to scam hundreds of women. The women all thought that they were dating him, when he knew nothing about it (nor did his wife or children)!

Internet scams occur for a variety of reasons. For example, syndicates in third world countries (such as Africa) seeking money, personality-disordered people exploiting others within their local neighbourhood, or predators using the illusion and promise of a relationship for their sexual needs. Essentially, however, the solution is to apply some of the rules described later in the book, in particular, the "90% rule". Do not allow yourself to be sucked into heart-wrenching stories. Finally, there are many people who do meet successfully online.

While reviewing studies into internet dating, one study of over 1,000 participants in the USA and UK found that a total of 53% of participants admitted to having lied on their online dating profile. Women apparently lied more than men, usually about their looks (in fact, 20% of women posted photos of their younger selves). However, men fared only marginally better. Both men and women lied about their financial situation or their employment (more than 40% of men and about 35% of women). The study did not examine similar rates of behaviour in real life (as opposed to online dating). In real life, it is easy to make false claims about work, but it is more difficult to fake an appearance.

In my opinion, online dating is more problematic than other types of dating. The computer allows a person to more easily create a façade because there is less accountability. For example, one very successful catfish was actually a woman who used a male persona to make connections online. Unlike real life, it is difficult to tell the difference between men and women via an online interaction. As such, every time the catfish and her victims were supposed to talk in real time, a technological problem prevented the call from taking place. Scammers might also utilise suitable voices to allow them to weave their deceptive magic.

This concept of creating false profiles is in some respects accepted by society. Police officers in Australia, for example, pose as children on online chat sites in order to catch men who attempt to sexually exploit or meet with that "child". The men think they are talking to children of 12 or 13 years old but it is actually a police officer. While such entrapment façades are for society's benefit, it does demonstrate how easy it is to create a façade online.

During a Family Court case in which I was involved, I asked the parties how well they knew each other before the marriage. They said that they had dated for two years. In fact, they had dated online and had typically spoken via texts rather than face-to-face. The man had come to Australia on two occasions for two weeks, and the woman had been to the USA for four weeks. Therefore, while they "dated" for two years, they had only had eight weeks of actual time together. During the two years of dating, they had not had an opportunity to go through the normal courtship "try before you buy" or to work out what their perpetual problems might be.

There are several important considerations for anyone engaging in online dating. The first one is to ensure your own safety, including not giving out personal phone numbers and addresses (not until you have had an opportunity to get to know the person in real time), meeting in a public place (and have a few opportunities to date), and ensuring that you drive yourself to the first date (so you don't have to reveal your address). I recommend that from the beginning you set yourself up so that you are not in any position of obligation. In other words, pay half the bill and do not allow anyone to "woo" you.

It is also advisable to undertake some research. This can include determining whether their name appears on any of warning sites and whether they have a legitimate footprint online. Social media can be helpful, as can searches of their image to see if any information appears elsewhere. Trying typing details from their profile in the search engines of other dating sites. In short, do not take anything at face value.

One of the most common ways in which people become the subject of blackmail is through the provision of intimate pictures of themselves, or by using a webcam to share sexual experiences (unaware that the images are being recorded). Once the material is in their hands, the scammers threaten to send the pictures to your other contacts unless you pay them not to. This threat is very effective, as most people have connections to parents, siblings, friends and work colleagues via social media such as Facebook. Before you start sending anyone intimate pictures of yourself, or engaging in online sexual behaviour, ensure that you know who you are dealing with and whether they will respect you.

I am both a qualified forensic psychologist and clinical psychologist, however, I prefer to think of myself as a cynical psychologist when it comes to assessing people. When assessing a relationship or looking for evidence, it is helpful to have an element of cynicism or scepticism. If you want to have a successful dating experience or relationship, having that healthy degree of scepticism will help. The easier it is for someone to create false evidence, the better it is for you to apply the cynical assessment approaches.

In the stories of those who have been scammed, abused or manipulated, a common theme is that those affected were embarrassed to talk to others about their situation. Therefore, it is important to have a trusted friend or family member to talk to from the beginning. They are far more likely to see a scam because they are not emotionally connected to the situation and, if you talk to them early enough, you might avoid higher levels of manipulation.

Love Finder Tools:

- ↣ The internet is a great place to meet people, but you need to apply greater caution to your dealings online than you would in real time. The scope for deception is greater. Apply your private detective skills and do some research.

- Scamming is a risk. Do not send money to anyone based on sob stories, to pay for visas, or help in other ways unless you can afford to lose the money. Do not send intimate photos or videos unless you are confident with your choice of partner.

- Take it slow if you want to have time to screen for risks. Make sure you have some real time with the person.

- Early dates should be in a public place. Drive yourself so that you do not need to be picked up and avoid setting up an obligation to the person which can be used against you.

Substance Screen

ANITA MET ROB AT A music festival. At the time Rob was the life of the party, full of energy and dancing all night. He made it one of the most amazing experiences in Anita's young life. They decided to meet up a week later to see a band in the city. Again, full of energy and vigour it was a star-spangled evening. They spent the following day together, but Rob was snappy and irritable. He said he was feeling tired from working long hours during the week, and Anita believed him. During the next 12 months of dating Anita sometimes wondered about Rob's variable moods. After five years of living together, Anita found a crack pipe. Shortly after that, she discovered that despite making extra payments to the joint mortgage it had been redrawn to the maximum. Anita lost her deposit, five years of extra mortgage payments and her inheritance of half a million dollars from an uncle. Rob was a high functioning methamphetamine addict.

One of the ways in which people can find themselves in a difficult relationship is when their partner is a substance abuser. These people are masters at creating an illusion in order to hide their substance abuse from the harsh light of the world. There are three broad types of substance abuse: illicit drugs, prescription drugs and alcohol. It is easy to say that you would not date a person who is a drug addict (living in a squat with needle marks in their arm) or an alcoholic (lying with a bottle in a brown paper bag in a gutter at the side of a road). Unfortunately, one of the tricky aspects of life is that there are many people who are high functioning addicts (that is, they might present well but can cause problems later). What do you need to look for in order to be safe?

Firstly, all three of the main substance types (illicit drugs, prescription drugs and alcohol) are mood altering and as such you need to be aware of wide variations in mood (in particular, alternating between being very calm, having excessive energy and agitation). It is important to know a little bit about the way in which each substance works to understand what you are seeing. However, variability of mood can become quite marked cycles: that is, a calmness or energy associated with the intoxicated state, irritability during the withdrawal state and aggression when the withdrawal state is prolonged.

Before talking about the individual substances, it is also important to be aware of behavioural indicators. The most common of these is deception. People who are high functioning addicts are quite remarkable in their ability to hide their substance use, whether it is hiding bottles, drugs or the activities in which they are engaging. The substance abuser is very clever at creating a front and telling stories. The key tool is to identify periods in which their behaviour becomes inconsistent in order to catch them out on small deceptions. People will make excuses. This is where, to some degree, the 90% rule (explained below) is useful – are these excuses plausible? Unfortunately, the 90% rule generally relates to the big things, but lots of small stories can become quite plausible without necessarily drawing attention. In that case, look at the frequency of excuses. In the above example, Rob was a salesman and had to attend meetings at all hours of the night (or so Anita thought).

Alcohol abuse consists of two broad patterns. The first is the chronic drinker who drinks excessive amounts on a regular basis. The second is the binge drinker who goes through periods of not drinking followed by periods of very heavy drinking. The binge drinker is often harder to spot because, during the dating phase, they are on their best behaviour and will not drink most of the time – the odd period of binge drinking can be explained away. This is where a discussion about past behaviour can sometimes reveal periods in which your partner has drunk too much and got into trouble. A significant warning sign is if your partner drinks to excess (for example, at a party) and does not seem to be able to stop. Obviously, the age of the person is relevant – a 21-year-old who gets drunk is far more typical (developmentally speaking) than a 41-year-old who drinks to excess and gets drunk. While both may have a problem, the 41-year-old is likely to have a more significant problem. The most common reason for binge drinking is to regulate the emotion or stress overwhelming that person – or they simply cannot stop that drinking pattern (which is why they go through periods of binge drinking and not drinking at all).

The chronic drinker (someone who drinks frequently and often too much) is more interesting. They need alcohol to get through the day because the alcohol blocks emotions – it is their day-to-day stress management. A very interesting study of the brain discovered that many alcoholics have an absence of brain activity in the Alpha frequency (a particular frequency of calm, relaxed brain function). Instead, their brains showed an over-aroused pattern. If a chronic drinker undertook an EEG to measure their brainwaves, relaxed brain activity would appear in the EEG after the third drink. It is as if the alcohol induces a brain reaction which is ordinarily lacking. Therefore, a chronic drinker drinks every day to feel a sense of calm. If you are in a relationship with someone who drinks every day, and particularly someone who consumes over three drinks a day, this is likely to cause problems in the future (as chronic drinking creates health, behavioural and other problems).

Methamphetamine is an illicit drug that is increasing in popularity and use. In my opinion, you are more likely to meet a meth addict than a heroin addict when dating. The heroin addict is reasonably obvious. Meth addicts are better able to fit in. During the assessment of a meth addict, I always ask them how they feel when they take the drug. The two most common reactions are "normal" and "powerful and alert". The meth addict who describes themselves as feeling normal often has attention deficit disorder (ADHD) (diagnosed or undiagnosed) – the methamphetamine activates their frontal lobes to help them feel normal. It would be preferable for such people to be on prescribed instead of illicit medication. They are likely to have a pattern of attention deficit behaviours, which could make your life like a rollercoaster. The meth addict who says that the drug makes them feel powerful is responding to the dopamine effect of methamphetamine. Meth, particularly crystal meth, triggers very large doses of dopamine (a pleasure neurotransmitter).

The ADHD type of user is quite hard to spot because they look normal. Often it is the patterns of irrational and irregular behaviour which will give them away. This will most likely occur when they are off the drug rather than when they are using it. The person who is using the drug to feel strong and powerful is a lot harder to detect if they are taking only moderate doses. These are Robs of the world. Rob started using methamphetamine recreationally and appeared to be energetic and functional. Over time he used more of the drug until it became a problem of high frequency. You will likely see periods of highs and lows or crashing on weekends for excessive amounts of sleep. Eventually, anger and reactiveness increase. Getting involved with a meth addict can create major problems in your life. This is because of the cost of feeding a habit, the aggression which comes through irritability, and the fact that the addict cannot deal with their problems. It is better to spot the problems early and leave while you can.

Marijuana is quite a popular drug. People view it as harmless and that some of its components have medical benefits. However, marijuana is also a drug with a dark side. In regular doses, it is absorbed into the fatty tissue (including the brain which is a type of fat). Consequently, heavy marijuana smokers often show changes such as depression, a lack of motivation and problems with short-term memory. People who are chronic marijuana smokers often, but not always, mask anxiety disorders. It is also interesting to note that, while amphetamine psychosis is well-documented, marijuana is the substance most commonly associated with admission to psychiatric hospitals for episodes of psychosis. The chronic marijuana smoker is usually evident from their general style. They tend to have a slowness of life. They often want to start the day with smoking and typically do not want to hide that fact. Being in a relationship with a chronic marijuana smoker is not an easy place to be because one of the common side effects of chronic smoking is the "amotivational state", that is, the chronic smoker tends not to be ambitious, driven or achievement orientated. If you are in a relationship with a chronic marijuana smoker, you will be doing much of the work alone (and possibly doing it all).

Prescription medications (for a variety of conditions) can be abused in many ways. Some popular medications which are frequently abused are benzodiazepine (relaxation medication such as Valium or sleeping tablets), opiate-based medications (heavy-duty painkillers such as Oxycodone) and many others. At an extreme level, people addicted to prescription medications might go doctor shopping (that is, approach several different doctors to obtain prescriptions). On any level, the person relies on their medication to get by. This can create a rollercoaster ride.

Common to all addictions is the fact that people turn to a substance, rather than to a person, when issues and problems arise. Therefore, during times of stress or crises in life, you will be doing it alone. Your partner, because of their reliance on a substance, will be functioning lower than normal. In general, the less reliant someone is on a substance, the more present they can be in your relationship. If you want an equal relationship, it is critical that you have someone who can be emotionally present and reliable. If you are with a substance abuser, your role will be more like that of a parent in a parent-child relationship (you have to be the responsible person).

One of the common mistakes people make is to believe that they can help a person with a substance abuse problem stop using that substance. While this might be true in a minority of cases, those dynamics usually create co-dependence – that is, where your desire to rescue is met by resistance and the two of you enter a never-ending cycle of helping and relapsing. This is not a healthy place to be. Ultimately, people can only change themselves. Rather than trying to change a person, it is better to find that person post-addiction.

The alcohol and drug literature uses the term "dry alcoholic" with respect to former addicts. This means that a person no longer uses the substances, but they still have all the addiction behaviours. If you date someone who used to have a drug problem, you want to see: (a) whether they can relate to you emotionally; and (b) whether they have undertaken significant psychological work to overcome whatever it was that caused the substance abuse.

As a general rule of thumb, at least two years of abstinence is necessary before considering that a person has overcome their problem. Someone who has only recently given up abusing a substance can be quite a risk for a relationship because you do not know how that substance affected them. That risk is especially true given that around two thirds of recovering addicts will relapse within 12 months (and most within the first few months). When first dating, an addict is most motivated to change. If they do relapse, you will then see another side of that person. You will spend your energy trying to recapture that brief positive presentation you first saw before they relapsed.

The issues with addiction also extend to other situations or addictive behaviours (such as gambling, computer gaming, virtual reality gaming, eating disorders, sexual addiction and pornography). Any addiction is a sign of an unresolved underlying need being met – the person turns to things, not people, when problems exist.

Addiction knows no bounds. It can be found in wealthy and poor families. Men and women can become addicted. Therefore, it is important to carefully check those you date for signs of addiction.

Love Finder Tools:

- Substance abuse is often well hidden by a person. Unless you look for the signs you might end up in a dysfunctional relationship where addiction causes significant problems.

- Evidence of deceptions and unreliable stories will often be the key to discovering whether someone is hiding substance abuse.

- Variability of mood states (especially when extreme), excessive tiredness after periods of energy and increased irritability are all warning signs. Note, however, that there might be other explanations (for example, depression causes both increased irritability and tiredness).

- Different drugs manifest themselves in different ways. The person most at risk is the non-drug user because they are ignorant of the signs. If you do not know anything about drugs and their impact upon people, it is a skill worth developing to add to your toolbox.

The Marketplace

During a trip to Vietnam, I was struck by the way in which goods of a similar type could be found for sale in the same area. Regardless of the type of product (for example, a Chinese New Year dragon, pearls, or tyres for your motorbike) many stores selling that same product could be found clustered together in the same area, however, outside of that area the item was difficult to find. The key to shopping in Vietnam was to find the area in which the required products were located – having the shops near one another provided the greatest range and variety.

Tanya, at 23 years old, was not someone who normally went to nightclubs. On one occasion, Tania's best friend was having a pre-wedding hen's night. After dinner the girls decided to have a last dance together and so they went to a nightclub. Tanya met Tom in the nightclub. There was quite a spark and a connection between them and, even though they had met purely by chance, they danced into the wee small hours. Following that encounter, they pursued a relationship and eventually married.

The relationship between Tom and Tanya lasted about seven years, largely due to Tanya's perseverance and her desire to try and make her marriage work. When she was subsequently asked to explain what the problem with their relationship was, she said that she found Tom to be quite immature. He liked to go out drinking with his friends, partying or to nightclubs and, with the responsibility of small children, Tanya did not want him to do that. Ironically, the way they had met was the very thing she now disliked the most about Tom. The way they met did not align with her normal behaviour. The eventual change to their lives after having a baby widened the gap. Tom argued that she knew what he was like and that she was trying to change him. He saw her as controlling and he did not want to change.

Like the streets of Vietnam, the type of product you get will be determined by the marketplace in which you find it. To put it in the simplest terms, if you want to have a relationship with someone who is a drinker and might have an alcohol problem, hang out in a pub. If you want to meet someone who is religious, go to church. If you want to meet someone who is active, hang out in a sports club. It is important to understand that the values you espouse will have a greater chance of matching your partner's values if you associate with people in a similar environment.

A well-documented fact in psychology is that similarity is an important variable for making relationships work. Similarities in culture, background and life in general make for an easier and more successful relationship. Therefore, you need to go to those places within which you can meet people who have similar interests to you. This is your marketplace. At the most basic level the two types of marketplaces are real time locations or online spaces.

The internet is a marketplace for dating and you therefore have to think about which website to use to advertise yourself, as that will help shape the marketplace (similar to the physical world where you choose between a bar, church, or recreational group etc.). There are websites which have a particular focus, for example, for brief liaisons and sexual encounters, for busy executives, for same sex attraction, or recreational activities. Obviously, different websites will provide access to all sorts of people. You are less likely to be able to develop a secure, loving and exclusive relationship if you meet through a contact website. You will have a much higher likelihood of meeting someone with similar values if you utilise websites that represent those values (for example, a website which reflects your religious values, or a website for four wheel drive enthusiasts if you like camping in the wilderness). Therefore, a key love finding tool is to find the marketplace which will optimise the likelihood of success. This could be in the physical world (for example, a bar or a church), or virtual (using appropriate websites).

An added complication in relation to marketplaces is the fact that people change with time (this fact has been discussed previously). The factors you value when young might not be relevant when older. Meeting someone through an adventure-based recreational group might be a good match when in your twenties. It is therefore important to view the marketplace according to your needs from both a "now" and a "future" perspective. For example, one of my passions is scuba diving, an interest also shared by my wife. Prior to having children, we would typically log about 100 scuba dives a year. After having children, and during the next decade, our dives were reduced to fewer than 10 a year. The impact of having the twins was amazing. Had our relationship been based solely on our interest in diving, then the change to our lives following the birth of our children would have caused a fundamental shift in our relationship.

Returning to Tanya and Tom's story, it turned out that Tom had an alcohol addiction. From the beginning of their relationship, Tanya was aware that he used to drink heavily. However, as time went on, she learned a few sad truths about addiction. First, addictions tend to be co-morbid. By this I mean that people typically have multiple addictions. To her horror, she discovered that he had a sexual addiction (which included multiple one-night stands) and which resulted in her getting a sexually transmitted disease. While the sexual addiction would not have been obvious during their dating stage, the fact that his alcohol consumption caused her concern should have been a warning sign.

Addiction can occur for a number of reasons but there are three broad pathways –early attachment difficulties, trauma or via experimentation gone wrong. Generally, people in the experimentation gone wrong group are the least addicted of the three pathways. People who have had a traumatic history might turn to drugs to dull the pain. If someone experiences severe trauma, they like to use heavy-duty drugs which anaesthetise (such as heroin) or prescription drugs (such as codeine). The last group is those with attachment difficulties. As described earlier, when people are young, they form their first relationship with their significant carers. If they have a good experience, they develop a stable attachment. If they have bad experiences, they have unstable attachment and problems in life develop. Those with a secure attachment turn to people to resolve their problems. This is particularly good in a relationship, that is, talking over problems and addressing issues with a partner.

Unfortunately, for those people who have an unstable or insecure attachment pattern, when under pressure they turn to "things" (not people) as a way of relieving their emotional tension. Those "things" take the shape of addictions, whether it's alcohol, drugs, shopping, pornography or gaming. They use their "things" to escape from the emotional pain.

During a relationship with someone, addiction issues will cause a significant problem. It is critically important to screen partners for evidence of addiction (as described earlier). Ensure that you do not hang around a marketplace in which addictions are prevalent. A relationship with an addicted partner is likely to cause you to be co-dependent and spend time and effort rescuing, rather than enjoying, a mature and full relationship. It is important to scrutinise your partner's possible substance abuse and addiction behaviours. However, an addict can become a master of deception and it is not always easy to find the evidence.

The key for you is to make a conscious choice to find a place to meet those who are positive and similar to you. You have to make conscious choices (refer to the earlier discussion about the brain).

Love Finder Tools:

- Carefully pick the marketplace within which to look for your partner. The marketplace should provide access to people similar to you in core areas.

- Screen your prospective partner for signs of addiction. It is very difficult to form deep emotional relationships with an addict and you will end up being co-dependent, spending time rescuing them rather than being equally involved and supported.

Try Before You Buy

―⚭―

IN PREVIOUS CHAPTERS I HAVE described the ways in which people can create a façade both in reality and on the internet (where it is easier to do). To see through this deception you need to be a Marvel comic character with some superhuman attributes. For example, Superman had x-ray vision (with which you could see through a façade to the real person underneath) and Wonder Woman had a lasso of truth (which would be particularly useful for you to uncover a person's lies). We need to achieve this, but we do not have superpowers. So how do you do it?

It is important to remember how the brain is wired (as discussed earlier). Remember that each person has a brain stem which controls basic biological functions (such as breathing and heart rate), a limbic system (the emotional arousal system) and the wrinkly grey matter (the logic and thinking part of the brain). When the limbic system is activated, the cortex is either shut down or in a reduced capacity mode. In simple terms, this means that when emotion is "on" thinking is "off". Love generates a very high level of feeling but very little thinking. Therefore, the strategy is to enable yourself to apply logic to the situation.

Evidence-based dating is probably the most singularly unromantic set of words you will read in this book. However, it is the most important strategy for you to develop to find the best partner you can. This evidence includes trying before you buy, checklist dating, and any other method that will allow you to see what the person is really like. Collect the evidence and eventually you will find the truth.

The breakdown of communities is one of the sad costs of a modern society. Over time communities have tended to disintegrate. When people used to live in villages (or small communities) everybody knew everybody else, each family knew what the others were like, and members of the community could be warned away from a manipulative or problematic person. The community advantage has been lost in modern society. Therefore, it is important for people to seek evidence about other people's nature or character. As previously noted, approximately 53% of people have lied on their dating profiles. It is important to discover, therefore, whether these lies are the more socially-acceptable "white" lies (to make a person look more attractive as a potential date), or whether they are lies used to create a false persona (for the purpose of manipulating and using others).

Data and evidence take many different forms and can be sourced through meeting people associated with the person you are dating. Some of the people I believe you should meet relatively early in the dating process include family and friends. Evidence derived from these people will help you determine the calibre of the person you're dating. This method of reference checking improves outcomes for employers, so it seems logical that it will also help you with your partner selection process. I have previously explained the behaviours to look for in a family, however, friends and even former partners are also useful sources of information. Family, friends and previous partners all have experience with the person, and it is harder for that person to lie when there are real people with whom you can cross-check information.

One aspect of evidence-based dating is what I call "checklist dating", which I mentioned previously. Checklist dating requires you to think about the qualities you want to find in a partner, and then look to see if those qualities actually exist. I believe that there are two broad ways in which people form relationships. First, a person chooses whomever is available (like I did with lucky dip dating). Second, a person chooses someone who is selected to a degree. If you do not have at least some idea of the characteristics you are looking for in a partner (for example, using a simple checklist) then you might inadvertently choose a partner based on their availability (or on some emotional and illogical aspect).

If your checklist consists of 20 items and your prospective date or partner has 19 of them, if you reject that person you will probably be doomed to remain single forever. No one will ever tick all the boxes. However, if you do not have a checklist, then the danger is that you will not be able to form a relationship based on qualities which are important to you. At the risk of sounding repetitious, I want to take this concept to a new level. What you must do is road test the checklist to determine whether the checklist items are real. If a person tells you that they share a belief, was that done to manipulate you or because they really hold that belief?

In a previous example, my father-in-law Jim said that he liked to travel. His partner wanted someone to travel with. Check. Jim wanted a boating companion and his partner said she was interested. Check. What happened? Over a relatively short period of time these supposed shared interests did not check out. The couple was then faced with discovering who the hell they had married and what that would mean for their marriage. The joys of a short courtship!

It is important to recognise that the item placed at the top of the checklist (the item carrying the most weight) will vary over time. The items that are non-negotiable will change with time. People in their early twenties often base their relationship decisions on looks or appearance. A man wants a physically attractive woman and a woman wants an athletic, good looking, man. However, women in their thirties often look for financial security, and men look for partners who will be capable parents or who will help to meet practical and emotional needs. In other words, the danger is that the checklist becomes complicated because we do not always know what is best for us both now AND in the future. The checklist needs to consider future needs. Meeting a party boy at 21 might be fun but later, at 30 years old and with two young children, you want Mr Stable not the party boy.

Research in the field of biology shows that the last myelination of the frontal lobes occurs at about the age of 26. That is, this is the age at which we attain our full adult brain. I used to say, in a tongue-in-cheek way, that men should not be allowed to marry before they reach 26 years old. This does not necessarily apply to women to the same degree because women tend to mature earlier (but not by much). Therefore, there is merit to not being in a hurry to find a partner. The person you are at the age of 18 will be very different to the person you are at the age of 25. The person you marry at the age of 25 will be different, but not as different, at the age of 45.

My advice is to "road-test" the relationship in order to see your way through these factors. The longer the period of dating, the greater the chance to reveal any perpetual baggage and to see the way in which a person reacts under stress. This cannot be determined by discussion alone – it must be observed. Obviously, a full road test (such as living together) will provide the best picture of what a person is like. However, that also creates complications with property, the relationship in general, and possibly with children. Caution needs to be exercised with the road test.

If you have a strong religious belief, then a road test is more difficult. For instance, you may have one or more chaperones, you might not want a sexual relationship, or you might not live together. That is all okay. This just means that it will take you longer to establish the true nature of your partner. You will, however, find it easier to remove yourself from the situation, than if you jumped in with both feet.

There are some cultures, religions, and even families that discourage dating as it is seen as inappropriate. In my opinion, this is the complete opposite of what will assist you to find a good relationship – that is, dating. If you don't date, you will not experience the way in which a person treats you, how they think about things, or how they cope with stress and problems – you will not know what you are getting into. The key is to date according to your own values and beliefs.

Irrespective of your belief system, when trying before buying it is important to note that you do not have to try everything at once. The longer you delay the sexual component of a relationship, the easier it will be to remove yourself from the relationship if necessary. Similarly, financial commitments are difficult to separate. It is preferable to keep expenses separate, rather than pooling them, until the relationship has progressed. STD (Sexually Transmitted Debt) is an expression from family law. STD means that you could end up carrying someone else's debt at the end of a relationship. It is important to note that there is a higher likelihood of incurring financially related issues when one of the more disturbed personality types is involved. These issues include a problematic relationship or a legal fight in the Family Court.

Some people are commitment phobic – forever trying but not committing. It is important to realise that trying for too long can also be determinantal to relationships. If intimacy is not increasing over time, then the situation will not change. How to access intimacy is an important principle which will be discussed later in the book.

It is one thing to say that love is blind. It is another to treat it as if it is stupid. Most personality disorders can be masked for months, but not years. It is important to see what appears over time.

During a plane flight, and while writing this book, I met a lady who said that she was fussy with respect to relationships. She refused to commit until she found the "right one". I like the idea of "fussy" – being careful rather than commitment phobic. Eventually she did commit. She said that she had been married successfully for nearly 40 years. She said that she had been the subject of a lot of family pressure to marry sooner than she did. As such, fussy is a good approach if you want to ensure that a relationship will work. I like to think of it as aiming for excellence, not perfection. A perfect person does not exist. You want an excellent choice.

Finally, in the course of my work with couples who had lived together for a long time prior to marriage, some of them said that the dynamics of the relationship changed after marriage. That is not to say that marriage is bad. It confirms that you cannot try everything. You have to give the relationship a decent shot, but it might still be wrong. Therefore, make sure that the marriage does not change how you feel about the other person.

In my opinion, marriage is related to commitment (which itself is discussed in a later chapter) and commitment is helpful for making relationships secure.

Love Finder Tools:

- Evidence-based dating is unromantic but critical. Conscious override of emotion is the best way to make decisions about new partners.

- Try before you buy sounds simple, but it is necessary. The longer the road test, the better able you will be to make an informed decision about what you are getting into.

- Delay financial co-commitments and sexual involvement as long as reasonably possible due to their impact on the relationship. Once in a sexual relationship, the harder it will be to get out.

- The new dating standard should be fussy, that is, be discerning and careful but do not set ridiculously strict standards which are impossible to meet. In simple terms search for excellence not perfection.

The 90% Rule

CONSIDER THE FOLLOWING EXAMPLE. PETER said that he dated Jessica for a few months before inviting her to go on a holiday with him to the UK. They got on the plane and she pulled out a compass and a spirit level. She said that the level helped her to not feel sick and that she used the compass to know where north was. Peter thought she was quirky. Quirky is kind of cute he said. She was a bit different he said. Now, hold this story for a moment.

Hopefully, I have sparked your curiosity in the previous chapters when I referred to the 90% rule. This is a really neat device developed by American social worker and lawyer Bill Eddy who, with his High Conflict Institute, has discussed many aspects of how to identify difficult personality types (particularly within a Family Court context). If you are a professional, or operate in the Family Court system, and deal with high conflict relationships, I recommend looking at some of Bill Eddy's work. However, the 90% rule is a good one for everyone to use, not just professionals.

With respect to the 90% rule, Bill Eddy asks: does the person do something that 90% of the population would not do? If a person with a high conflict personality does something, they will cover themselves with an elaborate explanation which you will probably believe. As a professional, I admire the skill with which those with personality disturbances can convince others that black is white and white is black. They are masters of the art. To survive this deceptive manipulation, you need to have a yardstick by which to measure that person's responses. The yardstick gives you a chance to compare manipulative claims against the standards of normal people.

As touched on earlier, people with personality issues are desperate in their quest for a relationship, whether that relationship is to use a person for their own satisfaction or to try and fill a bottomless pit of emotional neediness. They learn strategies to present themselves in the best possible light, but every now and then the cracks show. These personalities will then use damage control to justify themselves or try and convince people that what they heard was not true.

Returning to the story of Peter and Jessica. Applying the 90% rule, how many times have you seen a passenger use a spirit level on a long-haul flight? I think this hits the 99.99% rule as I have never seen it before. Quirky now becomes a red flag warning. Peter subsequently told me that the relationship ended because of the odd views held by Jessica and that he had spent most of his energy attempting to deal with the problems at home.

To use another simple example, picture a couple going out for dinner. A waitress knocks over a nearly empty glass of wine while clearing the table between courses. The male begins to berate her, stands up, calls over the manager (in front of all of the other people in the restaurant), demands another bottle of wine and says that the waitress should not be allowed to serve them and should probably be sacked. Throughout the whole episode the waitress has been very apologetic. After the tirade, the man explains to his female companion, in a very calm and patronising voice, that society is falling apart, service is not what it used to be, and people need to take responsibility for their actions. His female companion appears to agree with him, but at the same time is shaken by the intensity of his reaction. For the rest of the meal the man returns to being super nice and all appears to be forgotten.

If you apply the 90% rule, how many people would react like this under similar circumstances? If someone does react this way, how often would it include recommending the sacking of the person who committed the unintentional error? This behaviour is more common than the previous spirit level example but still less than 10% of the population would act this way. Ignoring the man's justifications for his behaviour, it is possible to apply the yardstick against his actual behaviour. Most people might be mildly upset that their dinner (which had been going well) was disturbed and that they had lost a small portion of wine. However, most people would probably not ask for another full bottle of wine or for the waitress to be sacked. The man's behaviour was clearly outside the 90% zone.

Similarly, in the example about Verity whom I had dated during my university days, she was unable to commit to the relationship or uphold her promises to spend time with me. While most people have busy lives and cannot keep all their commitments, repeatedly breaking a commitment and changing timeframes is not something done by 90% of the population. This behaviour should have alerted me to the fact that there was some aspect of her personality which was problematic. In fact, I got sick of the behaviour without actually realising that it was a telltale sign of something more sinister.

The beauty of the 90% rule is that it can be applied both professionally (in your work life) and socially (to the people around you and, in particular, to your relationships). Whenever you see someone doing something that 90% of the population would not do, that is a warning sign. The earlier example of the man who sat barefoot on the university lawn rather than attend a tutorial class, is about as classic as it comes for the 90% rule. He appeared to be free spirited and liberated but in fact he was not following common rules. Behaviour becomes a concern when it is outside the range of normal functioning. Everything that matters in a social life needs to fit within society's protocols.

With reference to the example of the restaurant customer and the justification for his behaviour towards the waitress, it might be the case that society has problems and a sign that the man is an independent, spirited, free thinking individual. I can guarantee that those same qualities will affect the long-term quality of your relationship. I can also guarantee that, if you continue with the relationship, the situation will change such that it will be you on the receiving end of a similar tirade of abuse followed by similar justifications for that outburst. Unless you shake the tree with the "No-test" (as explained in the next section), it will take a while before it happens to you.

You could argue that you do not know what 90% of the population would do. How do you apply the yardstick if it is a novel situation? I would argue that it does not always matter because if you ask others for their opinion the answer will be evident. If there is some question as to whether 90% of the population would or would not do a particular thing, then it is probably not significant enough to fit within the 90% rule parameters. There is, however, one very important qualification to this assumption. If you have been with the person for some time, the justifications for their behaviour will have distorted your ability to judge it correctly. In that case, ask your friends (if you have not been isolated from them) to determine how they view the situation.

In my experience with Family Court cases, disagreeing with the person over their behaviour results in punishment. Any friends of yours who offer contrary opinions will be neutralised or devalued, which in turn provides you with 90% rule information to understand what is happening, not to change the beliefs of the person whose behaviour is being analysed. The earlier you can identify the situation the quicker you will be able to assess it and break free.

The 90% rule can be applied to big situations (such a person telling off a waitress) or to a pattern of behaviour. The free spirited student is an example of a behaviour pattern. However, if someone hugs you too long and too hard when you first meet them what do you make of it? The first question is: is it normal for that type of person? For example, my wife comes from an affectionate family and she likes to hug. I come from an English family and I am emotionally reserved. In this case it is not the 90% rule as both behaviours are within the normal range. However, the question which begs to be answered is: is the difference too big for the relationship? Fortunately, the difference can be addressed if you can see where it comes from. My wife and I are still together after 30 years, and I am a bit more affectionate (remembering people change by degree not nature!). I also find that my wife is a good measure of affection – I think she is probably at 85% so it is probably an issue if someone hugs more than my wife would.

Love Finder Tools:

↦ The 90% rule is a yardstick to measure normality. If 90% of the population would not act in a particular way, then you have a highly significant warning sign.

↦ If the incident creates distortions (for example, continual justifications for behaviour), and these are hard for you to assess against the 90% rule, seek advice from those outside the situation.

The No-Test

A SECOND DATING TEST WORTH considering is the "No-test". As explained earlier, in the early stages of dating all the personality disorders and high conflict personality types will be on their best behaviour to create a good impression. If they are love bombing, being excessively nice or otherwise presenting themselves as Mr or Ms Wonderful, then you won't know what lies beneath the surface. This is particularly relevant as it is normal for someone to do some positive impression management. The issue then is to find a way to test if something is normal impression management (trying to look good) or a sign of a more sinister aspect of personality. In other words, what is the false front and what is the real person?

As noted, many people with personality issues have perfected ways of demonstrating more than just a good appearance. This behaviour alone should be a bit of a warning sign. To reiterate, if something looks too good to be true, it probably is. Therefore, if somebody presents themselves as "Mr Perfect" or "Ms Wonderful", this outward sign of perfection and being wonderful will fade and the person's true personality will, in time, be evident.

One method of determining the underlying personality is to either accidentally or deliberately push a button to see how the person responds. For the high conflict personality, the button is most sensitive if it is based on rejection. In its simplest form, the No-test is equivalent to you saying "no" to the person to observe how they respond. This forces the person into a limbic system response and the person will react if they are prone to do so.

The way in which you conduct a No-test is a little more complicated as it is often carried out with deliberate intention. For example, after the first few dates arrange to have another date. On short notice, cancel the date because you can no longer make it. A reasonable response would be for the person to simply accept that life happens, you are not always available, and circumstances change. The reaction would be a mix of disappointment and understanding. Disappointment is a good sign as it shows they care about you. Understanding is important as it shows they value your life as something that matters to you.

Conversely, cancelling a date will trigger a person with a high conflict personality. Somebody with a narcissistic framework will go into a tantrum as a way of manipulating you to change your plans. For them, cancelling the date is a rejection. The histrionic personality will create a massive drama as a way of forcing you to conform. In the heat of that reaction you will be expected to cave-in and do what they want. The borderline personality will become incredibly needy and unstable due to their sense of abandonment, leading to you to change your plans and ultimately look after their tender ego. The anti-social personality is likely to threaten you in some way because of your lack of participation (after all, you exist to meet their needs and your needs are irrelevant). You will be threatened, blackmailed or made to feel guilty in order to make you do what they want. If you combine a person's reaction to the No-test with the 90% rule, it will provide you with a glimpse of the personality type you might be dealing with.

All the personality types in the previous example will work very hard to convince you that you are wrong and that you need to change your plans to meet their needs. However, you should ask yourself how 90% of the population would react in the same situation. As noted above, a reasonable person would be disappointed and would likely want to reschedule the date, but they would not try and convince you that you are making a bad choice or that you need to reconsider what you are doing. They would not be catastrophically devastated by your decision, nor would they threaten you for abandoning them.

During the courtship period of the relationship, while the relationship is still relatively new, an adverse reaction will be tempered. However, when living together or married, any reaction you face will be multiplied by 10, 20 or even 100 times. In comparison to reactions in the early stages of the relationship, the situation will be intolerable when the person has control in the relationship. As discussed in the section on brain function, their emotional reaction will be difficult to contain once it has been triggered.

Doing the No-test may be contrary to your nature and beliefs if you have empathy and understanding. You may feel that it is not fair to play with other people's emotions. If that is what you really believe, I hope that I find you if I ever need to find a new partner. You are caring and ethical. These are special qualities which will make you a great partner for someone who will respect you but will put you at risk of being taken advantage of by someone who won't respect you.

Those of you who feel too compassionate to deliberately say no to someone probably do not have a personality disorder! However, it is an essential relationship skill to be able to say no and to disagree with a partner and it is perfectly justified to see how the two of you manage your relationship. In using the No-test, all you are doing is creating an artificial situation early in the relationship rather than waiting until later to see how your partner will react in certain situations. Remember that a child receiving good-enough parenting is taught how to repair ruptures in relationships – an important skill. As an adult you need to know that both of you have those repair skills.

If it is completely against your nature to manufacture a No-test scenario, you can simply wait for a naturally occurring situation to arise. Situations arise in life of their own accord, but they are real and legitimate (for example, cancelled events, work requirements or emergencies). Sooner or later you will see a No-test occur in your daily life. Your task is to pay attention to what happens and observe the reactions that take place. The danger in not setting up the No-test yourself is that you might miss it when it does occur in due course.

Consider the following example. Mary and her partner were on an overseas trip, travelling to many different places in South East Asia. At one point, Mary felt tired and subsequently caught a gastro bug. She wanted to have a rest day in the hotel to recover. This was a naturally occurring No-test. Her partner berated her for over two hours for wasting valuable time on their holiday. He told her that she could have stayed at home in Australia for free and that his efforts to make all their holiday plans was wasted. His response demonstrates both the 90% rule and the No-test. I agree that Mary should have stayed at home, but not for the reasons her partner expressed. Mary should have stayed at home to find a new partner who would treat her with love and compassion, not abuse. Interestingly, Mary and her partner married after this trip and were together for nearly 20 years. She reported that her partner's rages became worse over time, but she only felt that she had to leave after the rage was directed at their twin children. In my experience, this is a common scenario. A person will tolerate years of being mistreated, only leaving when they see that behaviour directed towards, and damaging, their children.

If you prefer to wait for a naturally occurring No-test, it is important to realise that by waiting your emotional brain might override your intellectual brain. When love kicks in the cortex switches off. You might not see the No-test when it happens. Furthermore, with the passage of time you might have a life with your partner which is enmeshed financially, practically or with the addition of children. At this stage the person is not going to let you go easily because they are emotionally invested in you and your lives are entangled. The naturally occurring No-test might be too late to be of benefit to you.

I would caution that the No-test should be a tool and not a weapon. If you use it intentionally once or twice in the early stages of your relationship to help you discover your partner's reactions to situations so that you can make life changing decisions, then it is helpful and ethical. If you use it to provoke a response when you know what that response will be then you are using it as a weapon. The No-test should be used only to test for the unknown, not to punish your partner.

Love Finder Tools:

- Saying no is part of a normal relationship. How your partner reacts to "no" is the critical factor. You can set up a No-test or wait for one to occur naturally. Is your partner supportive and understanding, or reactive and unreasonable?

- The No-test works by setting up a scenario in which you say no in order to examine your partner's response. It is a quick method for determining how a person will react, but you might not want to do something that deliberate.

Finetuning Your Assessment

CONSIDER THE FOLLOWING EXAMPLE. DURING a family dinner Peter asks his son-in-law Brian to stop parking his car on the lawn because it damages the sprinklers. Brian stands up from the dinner table and yells that it is a safety risk for his two young children to get out of the car on the busy road (actually a quiet cul-de-sac), that he will never come to dinner again and that he will leave immediately with his wife and daughters. Once in the car he spins the tyres on the lawn and speeds off down the road in a reckless manner.

In this example, Brian is reacting to the No-test and 90% rule, however, there are other things we can glean from this example. While the 90% rule is a neat little test to screen for inappropriate behaviour, there are five broad characteristics of high conflict personalities which need to be identified. These five factors come from the work of Bill Eddy and the High Conflict Institute mentioned earlier. They are thinking in absolutes, intensity of reaction, blaming, not taking responsibility, and extreme reactions out of proportion to the situation. These characteristics will now be examined in more detail.

The first characteristic is that high conflict personalities think in absolutes – "all or nothing". Something must be their solution done their way. They cannot analyse other solutions and if an outcome is not based on their decision the situation can become extreme. Therefore, during the dating phase of the relationship it is important to look for evidence of absolute thinking. Brian's comments about parking on the lawn instead of the street to avoid risks to the safety of his children is an absolute. Note of course that he drove off recklessly which is the opposite to the belief he was expressing. Never coming to dinner again is another absolute.

At this stage you know that when people are dating, they tend to accommodate the views of the person they are with. However, with respect to relating to others, it is important to be true to your beliefs and it is also healthy to agree to disagree when your beliefs oppose those of your partner. High conflict personalities will try to convince you that you are wrong and that they are right. There is no agreeing to disagree. For a person with a healthy outlook, compromise means that each person gives a little. In the world of difficult personalities, compromise means that they have lost something.

If you are still not clear on the meaning of thinking in absolutes, some common terms include "black and white thinking", "rigid" or "my way or the highway". This type of thinking is easy to spot most of the time.

The second characteristic in high conflict personalities is intensity and reactivity. If a person's reaction is in proportion to the situation, then you are on safe ground. However, if the reaction is out of proportion and, in particular, if the person demands that you feel the same way as them, then this is a warning sign. What about Brian's reactions? Yelling while at the dinner table and then storming out of the house. These are intense emotional reactions well outside of normal behaviour for the situation.

As a quick aside, one of the first things I teach people during therapy is to ask themselves "how big is the trigger and how big is the reaction?" If the trigger is small and the reaction is small, they are in proportion. If the trigger is big and the reaction is big, they are in proportion. However, if the trigger is small and the reaction is big, then they are out of proportion. Any reaction over and above what the trigger should have caused has come from somewhere else (either from past trauma or a personality style). Given that some of the more disturbing personality types have problems with emotional regulation (borderline and histrionic personality disorders, or the neurotic aspect of the 5-factor model), then the out of proportion reaction should be a clear warning sign of an emotional issue. Note that both narcissistic and psychopathic people can also have reactions that are out of proportion to the situation.

The third characteristic of high conflict personalities relates to blaming others. If I were to say that one of the most important traits for a healthy relationship is for people to take responsibility for their issues and problems, the opposite is also true. That is, that those who blame others for their issues are likely to have significant relationship problems. In the literature on high conflict personalities, a very common mechanism is to blame others for one's own problems. A concerning aspect of blame is one in which a person develops a "target of blame". That is, if somebody has a wrong perpetrated against them, they then identify a single person to blame and persecute for that wrong. This can persist for years. In the earlier example, Brian will take no responsibility for his reactions and will justify to his wife why he believes he is correct. In my opinion, the next steps in this scenario will be for Brian to blame his father-in-law for being unreasonable and then make it difficult for his wife to visit her family. He will use projection (blaming his father-in-law for any problems between them) when it is Brian who is making things difficult.

I have personally experienced a situation in which a reaction was out of proportion to the situation. A Family Court litigant lodged a complaint about me to the Registration Board. For various reasons it took about 10 years for the Registration Board to find that I was not a danger to the public and not at fault (in any malicious sense). However, less than four weeks after the Registration Board delivered their findings, I received a letter from the Board that the complainant had made a freedom of information request for copies of all of my records I had submitted with respect to the complaint. Therefore, the complainant held a grudge against me for over 10 years and then continued to try to have me held responsible. I am quite happy to admit that I made a small mistake, however, the reaction to that was well and truly out of proportion.

According to the Dr Phil on TV, you can either be right or happy. I quite like this expression as it holds a profound truth – that is, that emotional needs and logic might not be the same. The emotional side does not need fairness but does want to have peace. The logical side has to be right. The registration board complainant is a classic example of someone trying to be right and in doing so continued to pursue the issue for over 10 years. Had the complainant let the issue go, they could have been happier 10 years earlier.

The fourth characteristic of high conflict personalities is linked with blaming others, that is, not taking responsibility. One of the concepts I like to teach parents is what I call partial responsibility. For example, every parent has experienced becoming angry and shouting at a child in an "over-the-top" manner. I tell parents that they should make a partial apology, that is, tell the child that as a parent their behaviour (the shouting) was wrong, but that they were upset because the child had done something wrong (and so, being upset was justified). In other words, own the part of the reaction or behaviour that was right but apologise for the part that was wrong. High conflict personalities do not have the capacity to take responsibility, meaning that their position can always be justified, and that the situation will always be somebody else's fault. The high conflict person cannot take partial responsibility.

Extreme behaviour is the final characteristic of high conflict personalities. This behaviour can include breaking property, making threats to hurt others or themselves, and might include physical reactivity. In Brian's case, a good example of this is squealing his car tyres as he recklessly drove down the road. The threats and high conflict behaviour can be extreme, however, the person has the capacity to switch off that behaviour quickly (for example, if the police or a family member turns up) and act as if nothing has occurred. This is most disconcerting, particularly when the third-party leaves and the high conflict person reverts to their previous behaviour.

The ability of the high conflict person to completely shift their behaviour might make the recipient of that behaviour doubt themselves and feel like they are going mad. They have probably been told that they <u>are</u> mad – this just provides a further layer of proof. In psychology this is called gaslighting (after a 1940s movie of the same name). Gaslighting involves trying to make someone believe that they are mad when they are not. Normal people are not good at this, but for those with high conflict personalities it is a bread and butter tool.

In the case of Brian, his wife eventually left the relationship, but she had a protracted and difficult time in the Family

Court. Brian made several complaints during the course of the proceedings – to the Legal Practice Board about his wife's solicitors, to the Psychology Board about the court expert, and to the Attorney-General about the judge. Brian wrought havoc upon all those he believed were against him, and for a long period of time. This is a good illustration in relation to the targets of blame, as Brian claimed that everyone from the lawyers to the judge got it wrong.

Be wary of people who claim that everything is against them. This is especially true when people claim that there are conspiracies against them. They convince others to support them and their claims of conspiracy, and then use those other people to act as authorities. Those people who have been convinced (or "sucked-in") then become negative advocates who do the dirty work.

Love Finder Tools:

- The five characteristics of high conflict problematic personalities are: thinking in absolutes, intensity of reaction, blaming, not taking responsibility, and extreme reactions which are out of proportion. One or more of these characteristics should be seen as a red flag.

The Reasonable Person

THERE IS A LEGAL STANDARD or test referred to as the reasonable person test. The test is based on the premise that people should be judged according to the way in which a reasonable person might have acted in a given situation (that is, there are no absolute standards). In other words, how would a reasonable person conduct themselves, considering the circumstances and community standards? For the purposes of this book, I want to expand the meaning to call it the "normal person test". What would a normal person have done in the same circumstances?

When looking for a partner I believe that it is important to look for someone with the traits and qualities of a reasonable person, and that this is one of the elements necessary for checklist dating. What are normal healthy traits? In my opinion, there is a cluster of behaviours associated with the reasonable person and that these behaviours are normal.

In this context, if the reasonable person is the average, the 90% rule is really an unreasonable person test. If you can see rare patterns of behaviour occurring in only a minority of people, this will help to identify the unreasonable person. Conversely, it is also important to look for positive traits associated with the reasonable person.

In the earlier discussion of the No-test I explained that an unreasonable person will have an intense reaction whereas a reasonable person will react in proportion to the situation. It is certainly true that everybody likes to have their own way, but the reasonable person will consider the other person's point of view and their acceptance and understanding is evidence that they truly understand your point of view.

One of the first features of this reasonable person test can be found in an old Quaker proverb which states "me lift thee, thee lift me, and we ascend to heaven together". The beauty of this concept is that if you put your partner's happiness ahead of your own, both of you will be happy and your relationship will grow. If you are interested in your partner's true happiness, you will build a relationship that will grow with time. Therefore, it is important to look for evidence of your partner's genuine interest in your welfare (not simply telling you things you want to hear). It can be hard to separate genuine interest from the type of feigned interest seen in love bombing.

As discussed earlier, high conflict personality types cannot bear "compromise". There will be no compromise when a person feels entitled or needs more than their partner can give. Compromise means giving up something for the greater good. Couples with the ability to compromise are likely to build a lasting relationship. A lack of ability to compromise is a pathway to dysfunction. Therefore, if your partner jokes about "what is mine is mine, and what is yours is mine" make sure they are joking. Many a true word is spoken in jest.

Just as the high conflict person thrives on absolutes, the reasonable person can tolerate some ambiguity and accept that both they and the rest of the world are imperfect. A healthy partner has the capacity to deal with the fact that there is uncertainty in the world. Most people do not like uncertainty. It is hard to "not know" something, but we can do it. Truly difficult people will always believe that they are right – meaning a lack of uncertainty.

The emotions of high conflict personalities are either extreme or absent. The reactions of borderline and histrionic personalities are extreme because they react in over the top ways. A narcissistic rage is extreme as it is intense and sudden. However, indifference is also a common component. Normal relationships are characterised by emotions that are usually in proportion to the situation.

In a normal relationship, assertive communication works very effectively. Assertive communication will be discussed in more detail later, however, the sharing of emotions is one component that needs to be considered now. The reasonable person appreciates someone's feelings and will respond in an appropriate manner. However, the person with a personality disorder does not care about someone's feelings because they are only interested in their own. Therefore, people who can understand emotion and deal with it have a greater propensity for lasting relationships.

Assertive communication involves the sharing of feelings. It is a positive sign if feelings are mutually shared. If your emotions are not valued, then that is a fundamental sign of a high conflict personality relationship. It probably goes without saying that the reasonable person does what everybody else would do almost 100% of the time.

Problems arise if communication is not a two-way street and if your partner does not show respect and value your opinion. Good relationships are based on effective communication. Without communication I do not believe that there is a relationship. For example, I recently assessed a man in the Family Court who had a new partner from Vietnam. I asked what they had in common with each other as there was a 20-year age difference between them. He said that she did not actually speak much English but "she adores me". This relationship is destined to fail as it is all about him. The power dynamic is not equal. She will adore him for as long as she is subservient to him. This is an extreme example, but it highlights a key concept to look for. Are you equal in your relationship or is there a power differential?

The reasonable person is equal in a relationship, however, there are plenty of ways in which this does not happen. Equality is clearly threatened where there are significant differences in age, power or finances. However, even if people are the same age, the issue of self-esteem, education or culture might make the balance uneven.

The love finder tool here is simple. Draw a line on a page and put a fulcrum in the middle to make a seesaw (or teeter-totter in the United States) and then list any factors which are unequal between the two of you. Does one side weigh down more heavily than the other? If so, it means that the imbalance will cause problems in the longer term. I am happy to concede that there are plenty of working relationships with power imbalances, however, the greater the imbalance the greater the potential for one party to no longer act according to their own will.

There is a simple rule of thumb that an age difference of plus or minus four years essentially equates to the same age. As people get older (40 and over) the gap can extend to eight years. However, the greater the age gap the greater the risk of the two people having different world views, needs and expectations. Often it can take several years for the differences to become terminal for the relationship.

The ability to forgive is a final trait to consider with the reasonable person. Patience and forgiveness will always be required in a successful relationship because no one is perfect. Successful partners learn to show unending patience and forgiveness towards their partner. They humbly admit their own faults and do not expect perfection from their partner. This might not be easy to see but the ability to forgive is a critical trait to look for. There is no test, other than observation over time. The ability to forgive is most evident in the things someone doesn't do. For example, a person without the ability to forgive will bring up past errors in an effort to hold their partner hostage, they won't seek to make amends and they will seek revenge when mistakes occur. If you are holding onto a past hurt from your partner, forgive them. It will set your heart and your relationship free. A psycho will use you – you will always be apologising, and you will never be free. True forgiveness and acceptance are the keys to good relationships because a reasonable person has the capacity to own their imperfections.

Love Finder Tools:

- Consider the reasonable person. A key to good relationships is to seek evidence of positive indicators which will make the relationship successful. Are emotions in proportion, is compromise present, is there evidence that the other person's welfare is a genuine concern?

- Does assertive communication work? Psychologically healthy people respond well to talking about feelings.

- Draw a line on a page and put a fulcrum in the middle to make a seesaw (teeter-totter). Now list any factors that are unequal between the two of you. Does one side weigh down more than the other? If so, it means that this imbalance will cause problems in the longer term.

↦ Successful partners learn to show unending patience and forgiveness towards their partner. They humbly admit their own faults and do not expect perfection from their partner. Can you see evidence of this in your partner?

Getting Out

To set the scene for this chapter, consider the following example. Michael and Jodie met in a gym. In fact, Michael was homeless and lived in a squat, but he liked to maintain his physical appearance. His problems arose from a car accident in which he had suffered a major head injury. Jodie was in a relationship, but Michael liked to say hello to her when he saw at the gym. During their third meeting Michael said that he would not date Jodie, he could only marry her. After a few months Jodie's partner left her. She subsequently spoke to Michael and said she would go out with him. He reminded her of his conditions and therefore they got married. At this stage you should be able to see many warning signs. The relationship only lasted a few years before Jodie had to get out, however, Michael did not like the idea of his wife leaving because, for him, marriage was forever. Poor Jodie had to get out of the relationship for her own survival and for the wellbeing of her little daughter. This chapter discusses some of the key points to help you get out of a relationship (I can assure you that Michael was not going to let Jodie go easily).

While this book is about finding the right person, I feel that there should be some consideration of the ways you can get out of a relationship (like the one in the above example). If you are in a relationship with someone who has a formal personality disorder or a high conflict personality, at some point you will want to try and get out of that relationship. It is not good to stay with a psycho. Getting out of a relationship is something that needs to be done very carefully to avoid serious repercussions and, depending on the nature of your partner's personality problems, you could become a target of blame and your life will be made miserable. Your partner might become violent and hurt you, drag you through years of court proceedings or, if you have children, use the children to get back at you.

If you have discovered that you are in a relationship with a high conflict personality, you should seek professional advice before beginning the process of getting out. Note that not all psychologists have the necessary skills and experience with high conflict personalities to help you because this is a specialist area of expertise. Not all professionals understand high conflict personalities, so they might try to teach you normal relationship skills (which will actually make things worse and could escalate the level of risk).

In my experience with Family Court cases, I have seen plenty of well-meaning psychologists, social workers and other professionals tell a person to set boundaries and be assertive. While there is a need for boundaries, a sudden implementation of boundaries will escalate the conflict because high conflict personality types do not like to be told what to do and setting limits will only enrage them. To be effective, assertiveness requires that the recipient of that assertiveness cares about the other person's feelings. A person with a high conflict personality has probably never cared about their partner's feelings, but in the context of a break-up will care even less. Therefore, assertive communication will either have no effect or, worse, might increase the level of blame directed towards you.

There are, however, several components which can be carefully managed to minimise both wounding the person and triggering a blame response. First, a key word in all communication is "respect". Rage escalates when people do not feel respected. Therefore, it is important to temper your emotions, be strategic and demonstrate clear respect.

The second component of successful withdrawal is to understand that these personality types exist in order to be in control. The more that control is taken away, the greater the rage you are likely to experience. Therefore, rather than leaving, it is better to let your partner kick you out. You will need to give the illusion of control. It requires some careful work, but if you let your partner believe that something is their idea then they will more readily accept it. For example, if your partner says something that is close to what you want, reinforce how good the idea is to make them think that they were the creator of the idea. Therefore, if you initiate an idea it will be wrong, but if they initiate it then it will be the right solution (when considered from their black and white perspective). This allows you some leverage to try to move out of the relationship in a smoother and more successful fashion.

When managing therapy clients, a simple psychological method is to ask questions to trigger different types of responses. If you ask someone to focus on "feeling" responses, they tend to react emotionally. If you ask for "thinking" responses, then emotion tends to subside when the thinking part of the brain is engaged. It is important that communication is kept primarily on "thinking" rather than "feeling" levels to keep people grounded and to minimise escalation. Practice questions such as "what do you think about that?" or "do you have any ideas about what to do?" These questions require thinking and gives the person some control. Even the statement "tell me more, I would like to understand" is helpful. Avoid saying that you understand because, in their mind, no one can understand them (and you might receive their rage as a result).

At the High Conflict Institute, Bill Eddy produced a strategy call BIFF, which is a style of communicating with difficult people to maximise success. Whereas assertive communication involves discussing feelings and consequences, BIFF is based on providing Brief, Informative, Friendly and Firm responses. BIFF stays focussed on a particular issue and does not engage in arguments or discussion. The more a person can master that type of communication, the less likely they will be to trigger responses in the other party. Like all things BIFF is not foolproof but it can maximise the chance for the message to be heard in an appropriate fashion. For more information on BIFF, Bill Eddy's book called BIFF is available from most major online outlets (2nd edition, 2014, ISBN-13: 978-1936268726).

The longer you remain in the relationship, and the more involved you are, the harder it will be to get out. When you do leave, the high conflict person will engage others to help them (for example, friends, family or professional people such as lawyers, psychologists or government agencies). Those people will be actively negative advocates, who the high conflict person cleverly uses to do the dirty work for them (for example, through telling a hard-done-by story and then using the advocate's rage and energy to win a battle or court proceeding). The high conflict person will try to enlist highly qualified negative advocates because they will be much more credible in certain circumstances (such as in court proceedings). All I can say is that if you are dealing with that end of the spectrum, obtain good advice and I wish you good luck.

This takes me back to the purpose of this book. It is far better to avoid getting into a bad relationship in the first place or to get out early. Getting out of bad relationships is such a big topic that it probably requires another book. Hopefully this chapter will point you in the right direction.

Love Finder Tools:

- Trying to get out of a relationship with a high conflict person is complicated and requires specialist professional help.

- Setting boundaries will enrage the high conflict person, so pick your battle lines carefully.

- Showing respect and giving the illusion of control will help lower resistance.

- The BIFF method of keeping communication brief, informative, friendly and firm is very helpful for lowering resistance to your ideas.

Mirror, Mirror on the Wall?

I RUN A LECTURE ON family court assessments in which I begin by saying "for every pathology there is an opposite and equal pathology". That behaviours interact in different ways is a somewhat sobering thought. A relationship is in some ways like a big mirror, reflecting who you are back to you. However, it takes courage to look in the mirror.

The personalities in the relationship must essentially be some type of complementary opposite to keep that relationship in place. If somebody tends to have a histrionic personality, they are emotionally quite labile (liable to change). As such, the sort of person best equipped to be with them is likely to be a rescuer – somewhat dependent, passive and calm. If the partner was also histrionic, an unstable relationship would result because two unstable people would not last long. Therefore, long-term relationships are more likely if a histrionic person is together with a stable, calm and possibly emotionally detached person. Eventually, however, the emotionally detached person will find it too hard to remain in the relationship and will probably feel burnt out and depressed.

People who have a borderline personality disorder go very well with people who are passive and avoidant and tend to be fairly limited in their emotions (that is, they like the dependent personality types). At first the avoidant type enjoys the other person's emotions but after a while they become tired of the ongoing and unpredictable emotional cycles.

People who have an anti-social personality are often very good at manipulating others and as such they have a way of hooking into people who are somewhat nice. By "somewhat nice" I mean a certain sort of nice, for example, a person who comes from a sheltered background and finds it hard to say no, or who has issues which make them seek an apparently strong partner. Therefore, the anti-social personality finds people who are lacking self-esteem, looking for a confident person to be with, or looking for somebody to rescue. In any case, the anti-social personality tends to have a strong negative pull.

A narcissistic personality might like somebody who is also narcissistic, or someone with a dependent personality type. Two narcissists will not last long together as there is really only room for one special person in the relationship. Initially they bask in each other's success and use it to their advantage, but eventually they are scared by the other person's success and have get away from it. Consequently, the majority of narcissistic personality types are involved with people who lack confidence and who are people pleasers.

In the discussion on personality types I noted that the classic personality types are fairly rare. This applies to any relationship. Each person in the relationship has to have a way to survive. The greater the conflict in the relationship, the more extreme each party has to be to make everything work. It is important for you to consider that every time you make a comment about your partner's problems and pathology you should look in the mirror and ask yourself why you are involved with them and what your role is in the relationship drama. In all cases the complementary opposite allows the relationship to work. Therefore, you need to decide who you are and how you ended up there.

If the old saying that opposites attract does not really apply, then what principle should you be looking for? Psychologists have been studying relationships for many years. In terms of relationship suitability, one of the more interesting findings of those studies is also, in some ways, disappointingly boring. That is, similarity – not opposites – is one of the biggest key variables for relationships to be successful, easy and more effective.

In general, the more similar people are (in terms of their core beliefs and values, life experiences or religious beliefs), the easier and more successful the relationship will be. This is because communication is both conscious and unconscious. To illustrate this, when at university I watched a video in which a Texan met a Japanese businessman. The Japanese man would step forward and the Texan would step back. Eventually the Texan wound up across the room and against a wall. Afterwards, the Texan described the Japanese man as "pushy" and the Japanese man said that the Texan was "rude". What happened? It was simply that the personal space observed in Texas is much bigger than in Tokyo. The Japanese man would move to an appropriate distance which the Texan perceived as too close. It was the unconscious awareness of personal space which created the problem.

One of my side interests is a type of therapy called neurofeedback. It has been discovered that the electrical patterns of the brain have different frequencies which correlate with many different factors. One interesting study revealed that people select music that correlates with brain functioning. It has also been found that people like to listen to music which is in the frequency of their personality. From a dating point of view, finding someone who likes similar music will help you to find someone with a similar brain activity pattern. This is a pretty cool finding if you ask me. As a result, make sure you include musical similarity on your checklist. Ensure that the person not only talks about the music but actually likes it when you listen to it together. A manipulative personality will say that they like similar music, but the real proof comes from listening to that music together because liking the music is harder to fake under those circumstances. Therefore, add a music test to your assessment and make sure that it is a real time assessment to see if it helps match you up. Note that this music test is only an indicator, not a non-negotiable factor.

The greater the difference in people's backgrounds, the harder they have to work to make the relationship successful because of the conscious and unconscious understanding of rules. That is not to say cross-cultural relationships cannot work, just that they are significantly harder. The research is very clear that while opposites may attract, it is similarity that determines happiness in a relationship. If you want to have a good relationship you need to find someone who is similar to you.

One of the well-read books in my library is called "Getting the love you want" by Harville Hendrix. Although my copy is somewhat old, I have found the concepts within it to be really quite helpful (a newly revised 2019 edition is available - ISBN-13: 978-1250310538). Essentially, the author speaks about the fact that everyone has baggage and that some of that baggage is left over from childhood. We are consciously attracted to somebody but on an unconscious level the person reflects the unfinished business of one or both of our parents. Therefore, if we had controlling parents, we are attracted to someone with control issues. We then form a relationship with that person and seek to change them in a way which sets us free from our childhood baggage. This is also where the "I'll change him" mentality comes from.

The trouble with this is that if you have an unconscious attraction to someone, you might not be able to see it because it blinds you. Therefore, while it is critical that you ask yourself whether and how you are similar to a person, you should also ask yourself how that person might relate to your prior unfinished business. The more problems you experienced when growing up, the more likely this could be an issue for you.

For over 10 years, I have watched a couple of my long-term therapy clients through their rather unsuccessful relationship journeys. Both Greg and Samantha are attracted to people who set them off on an emotional level. People who tend to be high functioning and relatively normal do not trigger the emotional arousal Greg and Samantha both seek. Unfortunately, each time they are unconsciously attracted to someone, the relationship tends to end in misery. There is no simple cure other than to keep working on family-of-origin issues and, ultimately, to make a conscious selection of a partner. That is, to go against their natural feelings and force a conscious selection process.

Conscious selection means identifying the ways in which you and your partner are similar and, therefore, your suitability for one another. This is the evidence-based selection I have talked about previously – to override unconscious attraction – even though it is singularly unromantic. In Greg and Samantha's cases, I have observed both of them having greater insight and ability to recognise at an earlier stage any dysfunction associated with their new partners. My hope for both of them is that over time they will be better able to correctly identify the factors that will make their relationships work.

To put this into practice you need to go back to the principles of evidence-based dating. Think about the factors that allow your relationships to work and ensure that you look for those factors. It is a deliberate and conscious way of doing things.

Love Finder Tools:

- For every personality there is matching personality. Therefore, if you look at yourself closely, what does it say about you if you are like the other person?

- Complementary opposites work better than complete opposites. You need to consider the ways in which you are different and what you are doing that allows your relationship to work.

- Can you see how you feature in the relationship? What is your part as a complementary opposite?

- Do the music test. Make sure that you listen to the same music together.

- Are you trying to finish unconscious childhood business?

The Intimacy Ladder

INTIMACY IS AN INTERESTING CONNECTION. As we share deep and sometimes dark thoughts and experiences, we feel something. The emotional sharing of our inner private world ignites a spark which if fanned becomes the fire of love. In my opinion there are two quick pathways to love. First, through some illogical emotional reaction – also referred to as love at first sight – where something about someone triggers deep feelings and numerous hormones. Second, the reaction we experience when we share personal thoughts and feelings normally kept private. Intimacy is sharing our personal feelings with someone new.

Although outside the scope of this book, love at first sight is an interesting phenomenon with some really interesting aspects. A body of research states that we are attracted to people who look like us. In a roundabout sort of way, we want to reproduce (or clone) ourselves, a concept that seems to carry some weight in a biological sense.

Unconscious attraction sometimes relates to powerful biological urges activated within a person to reproduce successfully. Studies consistently show the strong attraction of men towards women who have the best hip to waist ratio for optimal breeding. There are also random findings such as people who make eye contact for longer are considered to be more attractive, especially if they look at the left eye. The significance of left eye contact is that it activates right brain responses (that is, emotional rather than logical brain functions). Finally, environmental forces also add to the feelings of love. One example from the science of attraction states that if you meet someone on a suspension bridge, rather than in a classroom, you will rate that person as more attractive and likeable. Therefore, love at first sight is a complex mix of social psychological forces and not just a random occurrence.

If love at first sight is not what generates the most loving feelings, then something else is at work. The process of building intimacy also builds love. This process is so strong that, in many situations where inner thoughts are shared and respected, feelings of connection and attraction are generated. The sharing process can even have an impact on other situations, such as therapy. Psychologists are taught to be aware of transference, because some people mistake the feelings arising from sharing their problems with feelings of love. Some people feel attracted to their therapist (and in rare cases the therapist feels attracted to them – that is, counter transference occurs). Unless such situations are carefully managed, boundaries can be crossed, and ethical or moral problems can arise.

To make intimacy work some support variables are necessary. These variables are respect and trust. Respect is needed because sharing is only effective if there is a feeling of safety. Trust is the lubricant which allows feelings to flow. Building trust within a relationship is a reciprocal process. Many people fail to realise that a relationship needs to be built on reciprocal interactions. If you share a bit, then I share a bit, then you will share a bit more. If you share and then I only share a small amount, the relationship will be out of kilter and the trust power dynamics will be significantly compromised. Unfortunately, the process of "spilling one's guts" also tends to create a bond with the other person. This then sets up a situation where one person is more vulnerable. However, if both parties have shared equally, each will enjoy the same feelings. A true friendship is based upon equal and gradual intimate disclosures to one another, such that each person learns similar amounts about the other.

With respect to relationships, trust should look much like an inverted pyramid or funnel shape representing the number of people you share information with. The depth is related to trust. The deeper down you go more trust and the higher you go less trust. At the top there are a lot of people who only know a little about us and who we trust only a little. As we go down the pyramid there are fewer and fewer people, but the depth of knowledge and level of trust is greater. If the trust in your relationship does not follow this image, then something is wrong. For example, if your trust pyramid looks more like a column then you are not meeting, or interacting with, enough people. If your trust pyramid is the normal wide base then you are sharing and trusting too much with too many people.

It is also important to realise that you have to work to make and cultivate friendships. I foolishly once said to an associate, who had a wide circle of friends, that she was lucky. She corrected me in no uncertain terms saying that it had nothing to do with luck – it was all about hard work. Cultivating friendships takes skill and effort. The key to having a big circle of friends is to work hard to build the relationships and keep them active. Katie, a friend of mine, held weekly dinner parties. She spent a lot of time planning each dinner party to ensure that she rotated through her list of friends to include everyone. It was a lot of work.

There also comes a time when it is appropriate to cease cultivating some relationships. As your circumstances change, you might outgrow certain friends (unless you don't experience change and your life is stagnant). In my case, friendships formed when working in labouring jobs after school changed in importance when studying at university (where I gained different insights). I do not intend to sound snobbish – it was simply a case of friendships changing when I did – things that had interested me previously lost meaning as I gained new interests in life.

Despite saying that there is a time to let go of relationships, it is important to acknowledge that shared history and experiences are very valuable parts of our makeup. Nothing is quite so comfortable as spending time with a friend with whom you have had some prior experience (even after 20 years or more). Whether those people are friends or lovers, the need for sharing is the same.

Returning to the theme of this book, finding love and not putting yourself at risk, another important test is what I refer to as the intimacy ladder. The intimacy ladder is not a single test but rather a way of looking at the process of building intimacy. In my opinion, one of the important ingredients for building a successful loving relationship is the sharing of personal information with a partner. Shared thoughts and feelings are very important for a relationship's progress.

Very early in a relationship, if someone shares vast amounts of personal information then they are likely to have a high risk personality. People do not normally share their innermost secrets with someone new during the first few meetings. It is not normal to talk about childhood abuse, an abusive partner or some other life horror within the first few minutes of meeting someone. Sharing is something which should evolve over time.

To illustrate this point, imagine two ladders against a wall, where each ladder represents a person in the relationship. Each time something of an intimate nature is shared, that person steps up one rung of the ladder. In a healthy relationship, each person shares intimate thoughts and feelings at a similar rate, gradually climbing the ladder. However, if one person is on the fourth rung of the ladder while the other person is at the top, something is drastically wrong and there is an imbalance in the relationship. In the latter case, one person is likely to have one of the more dramatic personality types, with an unstable nature, such as the borderline or histrionic personality types.

Another warning sign would come from one person reaching the seventh or eighth rung of the ladder, while the other person is still on the first or second rung (that is, there has been no real disclosure). This is a significant warning sign. These types of personalities are often very guarded, so they might have a paranoid or suspicious element. Note that the psychopathic personality type, who discloses lots of glib and superficial things which have the appearance of depth, will not have disclosed anything of substance about their real thoughts, feelings or developmental history.

When dealing with the more narcissistic types of personality, while they will often make you feel special, when it comes to intimate and personal information you might feel like they are trying to push you down the ladder. They will always need to be higher up the ladder – their experiences are more important, special or dramatic and, therefore, your experiences are not a reciprocal sharing but judgement of the process.

Therefore, the indicator for a healthy relationship is the speed at which both parties ascend the ladder. If you ascend at equivalent levels and rates, that is a good sign. It is also a healthy sign to go further up the ladder over time. You cannot have a deep relationship unless you share many of your deep and dark thoughts and feelings, disclosed in an appropriate and measured manner.

Feelings of intimacy and love occur when people share information about themselves and the sharing feels respected and understood. This generates closeness. The sharing of personal information is what separates a life partner from other types of relationships.

There are three broad areas or topics for people to talk about – the past, the present and the future. When you first meet someone, all three topics can be shared. After you have been with someone for quite some time, the majority of the past and dreams and hopes for the future have been talked about, leaving only current day-to-day matters to discuss. This leads some people on a path of serial monogamy. When a person feels that they have fallen out of love, it is because they no longer share with their partner. Logically, they believe that a new partner will make them feel special. When meeting a new partner, sharing with them creates romantic, loving feelings again and, as there is a lot to talk about, intimacy and love builds. However, this new relationship will also start to wane when the sharing stops. To keep those loving feelings, it is critical to talk about the everyday normal things in life.

When looking for a partner, it is very important to find someone with whom you can talk easily about personal matters and, therefore, this factor should be high on your checklist. Remember that some people are easier to talk to than others.

It has been well-documented in psychology that romantic love is a short-lived experience, probably due to this sharing process. Therefore, the speed at which you climb the intimacy ladder will be faster in the first couple of years of your relationship. The research shows, however, that couples who have been together for 30 or more years, and are happy in their relationship, experience romantic love to only a small degree. Their love is shaped by companionship. If you stop climbing the ladder, or even come down the ladder, then the relationship will start to falter. Part of falling out of love comes from not having the time or inclination to share.

In my opinion, the most important variable for a parent is empathy, and the most important variable for a relationship is respect. While empathy is important in adult relationships, children have the greatest need to be heard. Respect between adults allows them to trust each other and feel safe. If a marriage counsellor were to video their sessions, the way in which a couple looks at one another could be used to predict whether their relationship will work. If the look is one of contempt (the opposite to love and respect and a significant threat to intimacy), then that is a warning sign. Contempt is also evident when one person speaks but the other person does not respect that and, in fact, reacts negatively towards anything said. That is a toxic position for a relationship.

A final thought about intimacy is how to share your darker secrets. It is important to let your partner know that the weight of your past is something you carry lightly. If you struggle with emotional issues you might attract a rescuer. This struggle can prevent you from having a normal and healthy relationship. If the weight of your past is not carried lightly, then you need position yourself to make that possible. By this I mean that you have undertaken therapy to release the emotional burden of the past. The therapy technique of Eye Movement Desensitisation and Reprocessing (EMDR) is an excellent tool for releasing trauma.

It is carried out by specially trained psychologists, but further information on EDMR can be found by searching for the term on the internet.

The bottom line is that sharing for increased intimacy does not mean that you need to become a therapist for your partner. Intimacy can be damaged if one person places overwhelming emotions onto their partner. By the same token, a loving and supportive partner is a great asset during the therapy process.

Love Finder Tools:

- Respect is one of the most important qualities in a relationship. It is important to respect your partner to build trust. Ensure that you look for evidence of respect when considering potential partners.

- Love comes from emotional intimacy. The sharing of personal information generates love. If you want to find love, then you need to share.

- Sharing should be reciprocal and at the same rate. Using the ladder analogy, you both ascend the ladder at roughly the same speed.

- Those who share too quickly, or not at all, are risky people with whom to pursue relationships.

- You should not be a therapist for your partner. Seek professional help to lighten your shared load.

Assertive Communication

———∞∞———

IT HAS BEEN SAID THAT no man is an island. In my opinion, in psychological terms people are not designed to be alone, but to be in groups. We are social creatures and as such do not want to be isolated. Although islands have an advantage in that they remain unmoving in one place, making interactions predictable, I believe that a relationship is more like two ships coming together. If the course of one or both ships changes too much, they crash into one another. It requires skill to keep the ships moving along together in harmony.

There is perhaps no area in life more complicated than learning how to relate to others. There are many subtle rules to be learned, an internal sense of confidence to develop, and opportunities to seek – all built upon some underlying fundamental building blocks. The better the relationships within your family, the greater the likelihood that you will have developed good communication skills. Of relevance here is the previous chapter on checking out the stable before buying the horse.

I learned from hard experience one of the most powerful lessons regarding communication, best summed up in my "chicken dinner" story. In my late teens I was friends with a young married couple who I used to meet regularly. One Friday night I bought a takeaway chicken dinner for us to share. We had a great time and they were very grateful. The next week I did the same and they acknowledged my generosity. The third week I did it again and they said very little. On the fourth week they said "Phil, isn't it about time you went and got the chicken?"

At the time, as a 19-year-old, I felt used and betrayed. I had relatively little money and they had turned my generous gift into a demand. With the assertiveness skills I had developed to that point, I did the typical Australian male thing and avoided them for nine months. In my head I was saying "that will show them". In reality, they probably never knew why I stopped seeing them.

Over the years I have come to realise that what transpired was as much, if not more, my fault than theirs. What they displayed was normal human nature, that is, to first appreciate something, then accept it, expect it, and finally demand it. I had many opportunities to make a different choice. At week two I could have said "this week it's your turn". Even at week four I could have said "Hey, hang on a minute, how about showing a bit of appreciation".

This same process of human nature comes into play when dating. I recommend that you start how you want to finish. If you fail to speak your mind or stand up for what you need, then human nature will take its course and your partner might come to expect or demand unreasonable things from you.

For those of you who want to become a healthy partner and strengthen your relationship, remember the chicken dinner story and stand up for yourself. I recommend that you study communication skills to develop the ability to express yourself assertively.

Although this is not a book on communication, I will briefly address some very simple and basic skills to assist you. Simple assertiveness is perhaps one of the most successful things I have taught during therapy. I touched on assertiveness previously and pointed out why it can be problem for high conflict personalities, but it is still a useful skill to develop because it works well in normal relationships. The model I use consists of three main parts. The first is to describe the situation in behavioural terms. The second is to express feelings. The third is to offer choices.

Behavioural descriptions of situations are important because people can become side-tracked by blame and judgement. If someone said that "You're always late", it will be met with a defensive "No I'm not". However, if the comment was "You said you'd be home at 6.00pm, it's now 7.15pm" we are left with little room to argue over the facts. This also avoids the kitchen sink scenario in which the person responds with "Well, you're not so sharp with your time either". Stick with objective and concrete facts.

The next step is to express feelings. Expressing feelings with an intimate partner is the most important part of the simple assertiveness process. With a work colleague the feelings expressed might only be addressed to a small degree. In an intimate relationship the expression of feelings is the most important step. Feelings are easy to identify when described as "I feel" (not as "you are"). When feelings are expressed, for example, "I feel stressed and angry when you come home late", it is harder to argue about it. If phrases such as "you are" are used, then the other person might become defensive and assume they are being blamed.

The final step is to offer some choices or alternatives. My recommendation is to offer at least two choices of which one is the desired response. The reason behind offering choices is that people do not like to be told what to do. Keeping with the "arriving home late" example, one option could be "If you come home when you say you will, then I'll be happy and can respect your judgement. If you keep coming home late, we'll keep having arguments. Alternatively, you could at least ring and let me know that you are late. I'll still be mad, but not as mad as I am when you just turn up". In setting such clear boundaries, arguments generally cease quite quickly.

There are several cautions to note with assertive communication. The first is that when most people begin communicating assertively, they often become aggressive rather than assertive. Therefore, practice assertive communication in non-critical situations before trying it with your boss at work.

Another caution relates to human nature, that is, changing the rules can bring resentment (a topic that I very rarely see referred to in textbooks). It is often easier to be assertive in new situations than in long-standing situations because the longer a situation has existed the harder it is to change. Take the example of a "wonder woman wife", a 22-year-old woman who married and wanted to be the best wife possible. From the start of the marriage she did all the housework, gardening and cooking, expecting her husband to come home with the pay cheque to rest, relax and not cause too much of a ruckus about anything. After having several children, the wife realises that she has too much to do. She then complains to her husband that he is not doing his share and consequently feels resentment and anger towards him. This is now just another version of the "chicken dinner" story. It is quite reasonable for a wife to expect her husband to help, however, for the first six years of marriage she trained him not to help. She needs to realise that any change will require negotiation and action on her part. She cannot simply expect him to respond to what she now believes are reasonable expectations.

Having established how great assertive communication can be, it is important to know that it does not work on a select group of people. You guessed it – it does not work on people with high conflict personalities. The first of the three steps in assertiveness is to describe the behaviour. A high conflict personality cannot accept anyone's view but their own. They are not interested in your facts. The second step is to express your feelings. A high conflict personality does not care about anyone's feelings except their own, so this step has no value. The third step is to provide choices. Interestingly, high conflict people do not like choices because they believe that is an attempt to manipulate them (there is only one right way and that is their way).

The bottom line is that assertive communication when done well works for about 80% of the population. For a small group of people assertive communication does not work. If you have evidence of assertive communication not working, then it could be that it is not suitable for the type of person you are dealing with. Similarly, when assertive communication works it is a positive sign that you will be able to negotiate your way through any problems in life.

Love Finder Tools:

- Assertive communication is essential for building intimacy and trust. Learn the skills for effective assertive communication and practice them in the relationship.

- High conflict personalities respond badly to assertive communication. If you try it and it does not work, examine the situation but do not blame yourself.

- Start out as you want to finish. Human nature dictates that at first people appreciate what you do for them, then they accept it, expect it, and finally demand it.

Intimate Partners (Again)

THE EXAMINATION OF SOCIAL STATISTICS shows that relationships are failing, and divorce rates are spiralling in increasing numbers. Terms such as "serial monogamy" are used to describe people who seek one short to medium-term relationship after the other. There are certainly reasons for someone to feel trepidation about entering a long-term relationship, fearing that the relationship won't last. This has given rise to commitment phobia, where people are reluctant to commit for a first time (what I call the walking wounded, who have tried but the relationship did not work). Those who have tried and failed, and in the process got burned, are reluctant to commit again for fear of the same issues arising.

If you are in the category of the walking wounded, it is important to address the cause of those wounds. A therapist can help you learn so that you do not repeat the pattern. Similarly, there is still hope for you if you are reading this book because you want to find a partner with whom you can make a relationship work. You should be able to overcome trauma from a past relationship.

Another type of commitment phobia has its roots in earlier life experiences. This might be due to a fear of losing yourself, seeing your parents' marriage fail, or observing friends with relationship problems. Whatever the pathway, commitment phobia is an obstacle to finding and keeping love. Those who are commitment phobic either do not start dating or, if they do, they stop rapidly. Neither of these are good if you want to make a relationship work. It is good to face your fears and do it anyway. Consulting either a therapist or a coach can help you move forward.

The choice of a partner is perhaps the most important decision people make and this book is designed to assist you in this process. The following section is intended to help you deal with issues relating to you. We receive relatively little training in making relationship decisions. We blunder into the relationship arena and hope it works. There is a wide and detailed body of literature in psychology and related social sciences which examines the factors involved in relationship break-ups.

Children raised in a healthy family environment will learn several aspects of mate selection. In my opinion, the first of these is that a relationship is not a disposable entity and that it is in our nature to seek a commitment to a long-term partner. I believe that, like the Australian Corella, people mate for life and that we need to cultivate a mindset that a relationship should be an eternal bond and not a fleeting convenience. The further you set your sights, the better your prospects for making it in the long haul. In other words, looking for a lifelong partner requires you to look for different things than if you were only looking for short-term fun.

In saying this, I knew a lady who had already purchased her wedding dress and was looking for a husband. To say that she came across as too intense is an understatement. It is a turnoff to date someone who is ready to marry before you really know one another. A husband should be part of a long-term decision, not an accessory in a wedding. Desperation will not get a mate. Having a sense of personal confidence that you are able to live as either single or mated will make you less scary when dating.

I believe that you should be comfortable in your own life and in your own skin. If you are at peace and feel confident, you are likely to attract similarly healthy people who will like what they see and experience. This is actually quite an attractive vibe for many people and is a good way to ward off many of the psycho personality types who are drawn to vulnerable and needy people. Furthermore, if you do meet a difficult personality type, you will have the confidence to say no and move on.

Research into relationship success shows that there are several factors involved in making a relationship happy and lasting. When examining a relationship in terms of intimacy, passion and commitment, intimacy relates to how much empathy and sharing of emotion there is between the couple, passion relates to the strength of emotional feelings, including sexual feelings, and commitment is the degree to which the couple has decided to stay together. The literature is quite clear that the degree of commitment determines whether a couple will stay together – a high commitment increases the likelihood of staying together. However, intimacy has the greatest influence over the happiness of the couple. As discussed, the level of sharing in a relationship is an important building block for long-term happiness. If you share your inner thoughts and feelings with another person, then you will feel close. Out of this closeness love is generated.

You may ask what happened to passion. Passion is the icing on the cake. It does not predict whether a couple will be happy or whether their relationship will last. Passion relates to having fun times which are short lived. It adds moments of pleasure, but it is not a lasting function of a relationship.

Being able to identify the factors that you consider good traits in a partner will greatly improve your success. Conversely, a relationship formed by two people drifting together is a recipe for disaster. Working in the Family Court arena I have encountered many people who moved in with somebody else very shortly after breaking up with a partner. Unless you can clearly articulate which qualities you want in a partner, then all you will get is the first available person. Such random matching is never likely to be successful. It is for this reason that the checklist dating strategy is so important.

While some folk wisdom or beliefs are based on fallacy, there is some psychological basis for other beliefs and they are worthy of discussion. The first of these is the concept of a "soul mate", proffered from time to time. The romantic notion that there is just one person for us, our soul mate, is a seductive but false belief. I do not believe that there is only one person that we are tasked with finding (wherever they may be hiding in the universe). If there was only one person for each of us, and if someone chose the wrong partner, then at least two other people would be affected by that wrong choice. I do, however, believe that there is a relatively small number of people with whom we could have an easy and strong relationship (or at least a relationship with some work). There are also some people who we should never marry. It is important to work through the process to find somebody who is our best match – not the first near match. It is preferable to get it right the first time, rather than go through the agony of a break-up and then try to find the right person the next time. Note that you need to be in the right psychological state to be able to delay that gratification.

A second belief, and one I believe to be true, is that no one should enter a relationship or marriage with the thought that it will get better with time. To think that the relationship will get better is one of the biggest mistakes someone can make.

A third belief is love at first sight. There is no doubt that some people trigger an intense response in others. However, it is important to be careful. While it can be a real and lasting attraction, sometimes it is a connection which reverberates with unfinished psychological business. To explain this point, consider the following example of a girl who grew up in a family with an alcoholic father. Every time her father went to and then returned from the pub the girl felt a certain way but hated her father's drunken antics. As an adult, she met someone who felt right for her and, because those feelings might have been similar to those she felt for her father, she assumed it was love. Sometime later, when her new partner started drinking and mistreating her, she might not have realised the connection between present and past. She had waited for love at first sight because, when she had previously met normal people (that is, non-alcoholic), they never felt right.

In my opinion, a successful marriage is based upon three communication styles – a large amount of assertive communication, a moderate amount of passive communication and almost no aggressive communication. All couples disagree from time to time, lose their tempers and become frustrated and annoyed. As such, ruling out all aggressiveness is unlikely, but it should be minimal. To illustrate this point, one of the strangest referrals I have ever had was from a lady's husband who called and said "I've been married for 25 years and my wife has just left me. She doesn't know why and would like to work it out". When the lady came to see me, she was quite genuine. She really did not know what had happened. When I asked her about the relationship, she spoke clearly about being a devoted wife and mother who had done everything for everybody for much of the time. She had gone to Bali on holiday and, while lying on the beach, realised how miserable she felt and that she had given everything. In my opinion she had a classic passive personality. If someone gives and gives and gives, eventually they will feel used and resentful. She resolved the situation by leaving her husband. I believe that this was a case in which the couple might have been able to work things out, but the window of opportunity had already passed for her.

While on this subject, in my experience, after a relationship break-up one of the most common responses from a wife is "I've been telling him for years, I can't take any more", while a typical male response is "I don't know why she left. I know we had some problems, but I didn't think they were that bad". Consequently, men need to pay attention to feedback provided by their partner, and women need to make their feelings and needs clear to their husband. As highlighted in the chicken dinner story earlier, clear communication is important.

Love Finder Tools:

- Commitment phobia is a major obstacle to forming a relationship. Make sure that you know why it is hard for you to commit and then try to change those factors (either by yourself or with a professional).

- Free yourself from the wounds of the past to enable you to have a healthy relationship.

- Stop searching for a soul mate and search for your best matched mate.

Making it Work

To PUT A MAN AND a woman together, expecting them to solve problems, work together and live together in eternal bliss, could on one level be seen to be one of the great cosmic jokes. In so many ways people are just plain different. Those in same sex relationships must deal with differences between individuals, while heterosexual relationships have to deal with the additional differences associated with gender identities (and the corresponding physiological differences in each gender's brain and body).

However, on another level there is a perfect balance to the plan. Men and women are different but, in valuing those differences, a relationship is made stronger and whole. For a long time, the feminist movement has argued for equality and, in my opinion, it is right to want men and women to be equally valued. However, in arguing for equality there is a tendency for people to lose sight of the fact that it is possible to be equal and different. Men and women do not have to be same in what they do and who they are. Each gender needs to respect the differences of the other.

The differences between genders have been documented in many books including "Men are from Mars, Women are from Venus" by John Gray, or "Why men don't listen and women can't read maps" by Allan and Barbara Pease. To varying degrees, these books describe some of the differences in biological and social programming which allow men and women to function in different ways. On average, men tend to be more logical, rational and structured, whereas women tend to be more emotional, creative and able to multi-task. These two skill sets can work together in unison and harmony to create a balanced whole. When they do not work in harmony it can create hell. I am not saying that men cannot be emotional, or that women cannot problem solve. I am saying there is a difference in what each gender can more easily do.

How do we bring synergy to these opposing forces? There is no simple answer, other than to recognise that neither a man nor a woman on their own has the perfect answer, but together they have a range of available options. I might be practical, but my wife is emotional, sensitive and intuitive. I might think it is a good idea to send Christmas cards to some of our friends in need from Church. My wife will want to bake treats and decorate the cards to make them look attractive and sensitive. I might initially feel annoyed because of the added time it takes, but I always appreciate the effort because her "colour" makes the outcome so much better.

The process of making the relationship work can only come through constant discussion and negotiation. It is through careful listening and the assertive expression of thoughts and feelings that balance is ultimately achieved.

The field of couples counselling uses the term fair fighting – a principle that I believe should be taught to everybody. It is relatively simple and involves several main parts. For example, ordinarily when two people start to discuss something, they discuss it until they become heated. Once heated, they stop listening. In my opinion, an argument is a bit like talking to a deaf person. If one person does not initially hear the other, they start shouting (believing that the shouting will help, even though they are still not being heard).

In fair fighting someone recognises when a discussion is becoming too heated and they call a time-out (which entails cooling-off – not talking about the subject until the emotion has settled). The duration of the time-out can vary. Some couples might need 20 minutes, while others might need 24 hours. At the end of the cooling-off period, it is essential for the couple to come back and discuss the issue. It is unfair to simply leave the issue, because that prevents any sort of resolution. When people are heated, continuing to talk about the issue without cooling-off will only do damage. Therefore, I am a strong advocate of calling a time-out when things are heated, as long as the discussion is returned to after the time-out. It is important for you to see that a prospective partner is able to call a time-out in order to regulate their emotions.

Selfishness is the single largest killer of a relationship. The more a person focusses on their own needs and desires, the worse a relationship will become. This is where understanding yourself becomes critical. If you want to have a truly fulfilling relationship, you need to put the other person's happiness before your own. I just said something very scary, didn't I? To prioritise someone else's needs above your own. As discussed earlier, intimacy ensures that when people feel valued and understood, they also feel trust and love.

The needs of an individual at the expense of all others is one of the big myths I will discuss in more detail later. A good relationship does include sacrifice – each partner is concerned about the wellbeing of the other. A healthy relationship is based on interdependence, which means "I rely on you, you rely on me, and we both share the responsibility". Co-dependence means "I need you, you need me" and these relationships tend to have a very unhealthy aspect. An individualistic approach means "I get what I can out of this relationship and, when I stop getting what I need, the relationship is over". In my opinion, your right to be happy at the expense of anything else is a sad myth that leads people astray. Of course, people need to have their needs met, but it is not always immediate or simple. Obstacles do factor into long-term relationships (for example, car accidents, unemployment, financial problems and illnesses such as cancer). A healthy relationship works through these obstacles and comes out on the other side. People who are "serial monogamists" simply opt out when a difficulty arises. They seek an easier life in another relationship and, as soon as that one becomes difficult, they move on again.

Ultimately, I do not believe that an individualistic approach is the way people are designed to be in a relationship. I have always conceptualised my role in my relationship with my wife as one of interdependence. For instance, when I was finishing my studies and my wife was working, I did the lion's share of the cooking and cleaning. When we both worked, we shared roles equally. When we had children and my wife was in the role of a full-time parent and I worked full-time to provide, she then had the lion's share of the domestic duties (but I tried to take up as much of the slack as possible). We wanted the lifestyle associated with me working full-time and there is a limit to the ways time can be divided. There is no right way of doing this, other than to negotiate what is best for you as a couple and set forth on that pattern. Note that my wife and I were not held prisoner to past traditions, so we created our own roles which have been flexible over the years.

I would liken family tradition to owning a car. The car my parents had was great for them, but I would much rather have the car I now own. It is okay to change and upgrade as technology changes. Therefore, it is important to change your relationship style as time and knowledge also change. We are living in a different era and need to do things differently.

Sadly, relationship information comes primarily from our experiences when growing up. We act according to how our family, especially our parents, acted. If we did not like the way our parents acted, we might do the opposite. Instead of doing something the same as, or opposite to, our parents, we should determine how to do what is best for us. We should retain the good things and get rid of anything which is outdated or ineffective in our modern world.

Love Finder Tools:

- Do you hold the view that men and women are equal but different? If you do, then you will have a better chance of making a heterosexual relationship work. If you don't, then you need to look in the mirror and seek to upgrade your skills.

- Co-dependency and neediness in relationships are qualities which can lead to trouble. These things are not easily changed but it can be done with work. Professional help is recommended.

Happily Ever After

FAIRY TALES USUALLY END WITH "… and they lived happily ever after". It is interesting to note that in these stories the "happily ever after" is the beginning of the relationship. The reader does not see how the couple negotiated difficulties in life. I wonder how much of a princess Snow White or Sleeping Beauty were after their marriages, living with their Prince Charming. In these stories, there was no mate selection (rather a classic lucky dip), no courtship, and each had come from dysfunctional families. While this is somewhat tongue-in-cheek, clearly these relationships were not well selected. Even in such cases, people can choose to make the relationship work but the "happily ever after" is the beginning and not the end of the story.

Couples who have a shared purpose and meaning have more successful relationships. Whether the sharing is based on religion, goals for the future, savings targets, type of work, or aiming for and contributing to a united force, these couples are generally happier. Where people work for a higher purpose, then the relationships tend to flourish. Where people work for themselves, that selfishness is key to a relationship breakdown. This explains why having children can cause problems in some relationships – the couple's common purpose is not realigned (one person focuses on the children while the other focuses on other aspects). As a result, the couple drifts apart over time.

If you think that having a baby will draw you closer or fix your relationship problems, then you are sorely mistaken. Children are wonderful and definitely bring new dimensions to the relationship, however, they do not come already house-trained or socialised – these are life-long tasks for the parents. When couples have a baby to try and fix their relationship, it is a huge mistake. Babies are hard work, and devoting time to a needy baby takes time away from an already troubled relationship.

Some interesting research compared couples who had children with couples who had no children. Before children, both types of couples had approximately the same level of happiness. After having children, those couples had a lower level of life satisfaction than the childless couples. Therefore, children do not magically make a relationship better because children are demanding and require hard work. Furthermore, the childless couples continued to have an advantage until the children of the other couples reached about 18 years of age. Thereafter, the couples with children tended to overtake the childless couples in happiness levels, a trend which continued to the end of their lives. In some ways it is ironic that happiness escalates after the children leave home. This demonstrates that the process of successfully raising children is one of the building blocks of shared experiences which results in a greater level of happiness (once the pressures of day-to-day demands have gone).

The research also clearly shows that, as time goes on, successful couples tend to argue less (however, this only comes through the assertive communication style discussed earlier). As noted previously, it is important to disagree but to do so with dignity. The love finder tool of greatest value here is to ensure that you disagree in a healthy fashion. Road-testing relationships allows you to see whether you can disagree when necessary. If you or your partner always agree, then something is not right. Conversely, if you never agree, or everything is a big drama, you have a significant problem.

On the subject of fidelity (which will be addressed in a later chapter), concepts such as open relationships, polyamorous relationships and secret affairs exist. I have yet to meet a couple who engage in such practices who have managed to have a successful and happy long-term relationship. These things fulfill short-term needs, usually of only one person in the relationship. The other partner passively agrees to keep the peace and therefore keep their partner. The relationship lasts until it reaches a point beyond which they can no longer cope, and problems emerge. In my opinion, fidelity, whether emotional or sexual, is an important building block for a successful relationship. Where people do not have fidelity in the relationship, trust, jealousy and insecurity will inevitably creep in.

Two expressions I have heard are "happy wife, happy life" and "if you want a happy relationship then set your expectations low" (apparently attributed to Warren Buffett). Both pieces of advice highlight some important elements in the relationship equation. The first concerns not being selfish and focussing on your partner's happiness. If your partner is happy then your relationship will be easier. If a relationship is only based on what one person wants, then it will be difficult to keep the other person involved.

The second piece of advice is quite profound and teaches us that our sense of inadequacy or regret in a relationship is often of our own making. The higher our expectations, the greater the probability that we will be unhappy. If our needs are simple, then it is easier for the other person to meet them.

For people with high expectations, the companion beliefs relate to mind reading and unrealistic expectations. We expect that the other person is going to know what we need and will provide it to us. In my opinion, the responsibility in this is simple. If you tell someone what you need in a way that they can understand, then they have a chance to meet that need. However, if you "expect" someone to know what you need then you are a failed communicator. Mind reading is an easy way to cause problems. Even if someone should know what you need, they will never get it right all the time. During therapy I take clients one step further – if you do not tell the other person what you need, then it is on your head if a problem arises. Conversely, if you do tell the other person what you need, then it is on their head if those needs aren't met. If someone does not know, then they cannot do anything about it.

If you want to ensure a "happily ever after", it is important to realise that a relationship is an investment. Good investments require analysis and ongoing review. Sometimes investments have rapid returns. At other times an investment might fall in value. It is the same with relationships. The goal is the long-term return, not the immediate return. If you work on creating time with your partner, then there is a greater chance that your relationship will survive. If you and your partner become too busy in your own lives (especially if you have children and tend to lose yourselves in that busy life) then in the process you could lose your relationship.

People have varying philosophies in life. These can range from the more religiously-orientated view (that our time upon this world is a crucible of testing, and trials are a necessary part of that experience), to those of a more worldly perspective (where "life is a bitch and then you die"). Irrespective of your beliefs, it is an inevitable fact that there will be trials, complications and difficulties in your life. When in a relationship, trials can come in many different forms. These trials can be external (natural disasters or extended family issues), added to the relationship (illness, mental health problems, unemployment, injuries and accidents), or of someone's own making (gambling, having an affair, using drugs and so forth). While every trial is unique and different, the common element is that it produces a massive amount of stress on the relationship.

The research shows that when people have trials there is an initial alarm stage (where they action against it), resistance (while they get used to it) and eventually exhaustion. This exhaustion might manifest as depression or another type of serious problem. The so-called "weakest link in the chain" is the one which breaks. When people become coloured by depression, whether that results from mental or physical issues, they see the world in a negative light. In something like 50% of relationship break-ups, one or both partners can suffer from the symptoms of depression. This depression might be in reaction to the break-up, but most commonly exists prior to the break-up.

A healthy relationship can deal with the trials of life, and people have methods and abilities to cope. The psychological term for people who are able to weather life's storms is "resilient". Resilience is an incredibly important quality in a partner, as is an understanding of mental health issues.

With respect to depression, one of the most important things to understand is that people's perceptions are skewed in the negative. When in a depressed state, all things seem negative and therefore relationships might be viewed in the same light. Some people leave a relationship believing that it is the cause of the problem. Had they treated the depression and "hung in there", they might have seen that the relationship was not at fault. Therefore, if you are in a relationship and suffering depression, it is best to wait until the depression is resolved before making the decision to leave.

The ability to deal with trials is important for making relationships work. Unlike the No-test where there is an immediate reaction, there is no simple test for resilience in your prospective partner. However, one source of information is to look at a person's past to see how they have dealt with problems previously. People who run from difficult situations are likely to abandon you when the going gets tough. However, people who have dealt with adversity and stuck with it are more likely to show the pattern of "when the going gets tough, the tough get going".

A second thing to look for in a partner to help weather life's storms with you, is whether they have empathy. Are they sensitive to the plight of others and to you? Empathy is key. Empathy does not mean "I have to know what you're going through". Empathy means "I'd like to try and understand what you're going through". A person who is keen to understand how you feel is likely to be a good partner. Someone who does not understand how you feel, or does not care how you feel, is destined to create a disaster. A lack of empathy is a warning sign that you have found a psycho.

Love Finder Tools:

- ↣ Respect is a key element for building good relationships, and contempt a solid indicator that things will not work out. Contempt is often not evident until the relationship has lasted a long time. Respect should be present from the beginning. Are you respected?

- Having a baby is not a way to make a relationship better. It adds work and stress rather than magically transforming the relationship.

- Look for signs of empathy. Is the person willing to try and understand how you feel?

- How has the person dealt with trials and traumas in the past? Is there evidence of resilience?

- Is the person someone who seeks to resolve issues, or do they run from problems?

After the Affair

THERE IS A FOLK STORY about a man who was the village liar, who told lies about almost everything. Over time, more and more people would not talk to him. Eventually he went to see the sage who lived in small hut at the edge of the forest. After the village liar explained his predicament, the sage told him that for every person he had wronged, he had to collect a white feather and put it on the doorstep of that person's home. The sage then told him to return the following night for further instructions. With humble obedience the man did as he had been told. Upon returning to the sage, he received new instructions. He was told to go and collect the feathers. The man replied in despair that the east wind would have blown all the feathers away. The sage then explained that it is the same with trust.

Good relationships are built on trust. Trust is easy to initiate but very hard to repair once it has been damaged. It is important for a relationship to be based on good values, which allows trust to build. Over the years I have seen many relationships in which couples have tried a variety of alternative strategies, from polyamorous relationships to "open relationships", to more clandestine actions such as affairs (both literal and online). In every case, these strategies threatened the core of what makes a relationship special – the unique connection between two people. Usually such people are looking outward because they are trying to have their cake and eat it too.

In relation to online romances or relationships, the situation can be problematic even if the people never meet face-to-face. During therapy a husband told me that, because he was not having sex with the women he talked to online, his partner should not be upset. He could not see that emotional infidelity can be as painful as sexual infidelity. He had been pouring his heart out to a lady online and, in the process, had told her several things that his wife of 12 years did not know about him. His wife was very upset, but he did not understand why. Someone who gives their heart, even if they are not giving their body, is fundamentally violating the intimacy bond. If there has been some emotional infidelity, then there are likely to be significant implications for the couple.

In my opinion, false accusations of infidelity are also very interesting. One person might accuse another for a variety of reasons, even when there is no affair. In this situation, there are a number of important points to look for. The accusations most commonly arise due to the insecurity of the blamer, or to projection or control. The accusations might also arise because the accused person does not understand the messages within the relationship. Let me explain all three of these situations. People accuse their partners of affairs when they feel insecure, causing them to experience jealousy. If someone feels that their partner is "not in the same pay grade", they become fearful of losing their partner. Ironically, the more they accuse their partner, the more they will drive them away.

The second reason for making false accusations is a lot more sinister and relates to projection or control. To understand projection, it is important to know that the basic psychological roots of projection come from paranoia. If someone is fearful, they accuse their partner of doing the very thing they themselves fear being caught doing. It is often the case that the first allegation is made when the accuser has started their own affair. If the accuser blames their partner, it acts as a distraction from their own wrongdoing. If your partner is accusing you of an affair, my advice is to do some clandestine research for evidence of their own wrongdoing. What does their phone or computer say about their activities?

The third reason for making an accusation of an affair is that sometimes people do not understand the messages they send. There is good research, for example, that people with autism are vulnerable to exploitation because they think they are being friendly, but the other person perceives the actions of the autistic person as sexual. It is important to apply the 90% rule here to see whether the accusation is justified or if there is a skills deficit. Note that this is the least common basis for such accusations.

The control aspect of accusations is a marker for personality disturbances. If you are wrongly accused, it might have been done to hold you in a lower position. While you try to prove that you are not guilty, the accuser has the upper hand and therefore control. In all cases, being falsely accused is a significant neon warning sign. In the early stages of dating it might not be obvious. It could be indicated by your partner repeatedly checking up on you, sending you ten texts a day asking where you are and what you are doing (always in the context of asking because they care) or accusing you of talking to the wrong person. The controlling behaviour starts in these ways but eventually results with friends and family cut off from you, past photo albums discarded, or possibly an alteration to the way you dress when you go out. It is a serious problem and by the time you realise it you will be too damaged to do much about it.

In my work with couples I have found that relationship repair is nearly impossible when there have been either real or imagined affairs. First, for a partner to cheat, they will have developed justifications to explain why it happened and they will place the blame elsewhere. Funny how this is starting to sound like the characteristics of high conflict personalities discussed earlier – people who feel that they are entitled to have their needs met and who can justify their actions.

To illustrate the higher end of personality disorders, I was once involved in case in which a person had a wife in one town, a mistress in another town, and a girlfriend in both towns. He had multiple children from these relationships and short-term affairs. He was a high-end medical professional and he justified his behaviour completely. The underlying issues showed significant deficits in intimacy and very strong elements of entitlement.

Second, for the relationship to reach the point at which someone cheats, there must be some fundamental issues in either the relationship or one of the partners. It has been said that men have affairs for sex, and women for love. While nothing is ever simple, it is important to reflect on the issues that allowed the situation to get to that point. Apply the 90% rule to help determine whether something was a real problem or if blame was being misapplied.

I am asked how a person can trust again. The partner now says all the right things and is suitably repentant. However, there is a level of trust in a relationship and once it has been violated it can never return to the previous state. Just like the folk story outlined at the start of this chapter, you cannot get the feathers back after the wind has blown them away. If you are in the courtship phase, my advice is to move on rather than try to repair the relationship. If you are trying to make a committed relationship work, it is not so easy. It will take significant soul-searching to be able to repair the relationship.

A standard in criminal law is innocent until proven guilty. Once trust has been violated, the burden of proof is on the perpetrator to prove that they are innocent. Prior to an affair, if a person arrives home late the assumption is that they were at work. After an affair, if a person arrives home late the assumption is either that they have done something, or they cannot be trusted. This is a hard way to live.

The proof I suggest people look for is in emotions, not words or actions. If the perpetrator undergoes therapy and changes emotionally then there is some possibility of the relationship surviving. These changes are neither quick nor easy because the burden of responsibility is on the perpetrator who feels justified in their actions.

Something else to be aware of is a relationship which starts as an affair. A person will say that their partner is failing to meet their needs, and they will justify their reasons for believing you are special. It all sounds plausible and the relationship seems so good. However, there are some factors which might destroy the new relationship. If this person can cheat on their current partner, then they can also cheat on you. While they claim you are different, it is a sad reality that the best predictor of future behaviour is past behaviour. Added to this mix, someone who has an affair not only has the capacity to cheat, they are also deceiving their current partner and are focussed on their own needs. This seems like a trilogy of risk factors which might cause you heartache.

Love Finder Tools:

- Affairs during courtship are a negative indicator for the prospect of the relationship working. If an affair happens, there will be a loss of trust which at some point will cause further problems in the relationship.

- While affairs happen for many reasons, they are frequently an indicator of a difficult personality who wants their own needs met and will lie and cheat to cover their tracks.

- False accusations of affairs, jealousy, or monitoring movements and social relationships are all indicators of potential high conflict personalities.

- The only indicator to provide hope of change is evidence of emotional change. Has the person sought psychological help and changed their way of dealing with emotions?

- If your relationship starts as an affair, your partner has the capacity to deceive, to be unfaithful, and focus on their own needs. These are all neon lights flashing a warning sign that you might be next.

I Believe in Love

As this book draws to a close, I want you to know that I believe in love. Love would have to be one of my favourite emotions. I can still remember the crush I had as a 12-year-old. I do not think I slept for three nights as I pined for my love, Alanna, who did not know anything about how I was feeling. Nothing came of my crush and to this day she would not know that I harboured such intense feelings for her. At the time I neither knew what those feelings signified, nor did I understand them. These feelings lasted for months in a mild form and weeks in an intense form. It was a crush in every sense of the word.

My subsequent experiences in love and relationships, including the passion I felt when I met my wife 30 years ago, have been amazing. Even today I still experience a wave of romantic love flooding over me as I look at my wife. Mostly we have the more staid but predictable friendship type of love, but romantic love can still fire up at times. Even the friendship type of love can wax and wane depending on whether we are busy or take the time to feed it with attention to each other. I can confirm that marriage is hard work but worth it with the right person.

In previous chapters, I provided personal examples of some of my earlier dating experiences with people who did not remain in my life. While some of those relationship break-ups were gut wrenchingly sad at the time, I have no regrets. All those experiences helped me to get to the position where, when I met Bethwyn, I was ready to take an active lead. They helped me to learn what I needed to do, and I was prepared and skilled to do it with her (she may laugh at my use of the word "skilled" but at least I was not entirely naïve and incompetent). Past failed relationships are teaching moments and, as long as you get out of those relationships early and intact (or at least can repair yourself after getting out), then the experiences are necessary and useful. Hopefully this book will help you to avoid having too many learning experiences and speed up the process of finding the right partner.

In my opinion, it is not only important to find the right partner, you also need to learn to be the sort of partner who can make a relationship work. See the shift here? This is not just about the other person. Maybe you are the psycho, not them. That would be a bitter pill to swallow. Note that, in general, psychos lack the ability to reflect upon their own behaviour. They will not read this book to learn how to find a partner (although they might read it to improve their skills in manipulating partners!). The mirror we use on ourselves is not a true reflector but a distorted image. If your distorted image leads you to think that you have been the psycho in your past relationships, then your task is to undergo therapy to help you learn how to operate in a relationship. Even if you are only a little bit psycho you have a responsibility to improve yourself. You need to be sure that you can be the best partner possible which is something that can only come from you, never from your partner.

Ironically, the best formula for success in a relationship is if there are two people who are both trying to please and help one another. At the most basic level, you cannot change your partner – only yourself. The more mature you are psychologically speaking, the better you can relate to others. Psychologically mature people are more open and less defensive. They are not jealous. They are proactive, not reactive. If these characteristics do not apply to you, try some therapy to sort yourself out. If you find yourself saying "they pushed my buttons, that why I reacted" then you have a lot of work to do! Blaming others and not taking responsibility are signs of a psychological makeup that is not very mature.

If you are young and just starting out, have hope. There are decent, stable people available – you just have to go out there and find them. Armed with the love finder toolbox you can sift the wheat from the chaff, the forever partner from the psycho. It is now up to you to action this process, assess and look for someone. I reiterate that your goal is not to find a perfect person, as there is no such creature on earth. Rather your quest is to find someone who has a set of problems you can live with.

As a young person you don't want to hear that there are plenty of fish in the sea. However, the age group of 18 to 30 years includes the greatest number of single and available people. During this period more and more people pair off, shrinking the pool. Those people who can make their relationship work will no longer be in the pool (except if something takes their partners). Those people who are unable to make their relationship work will continue to re-enter the pool. Therefore, the quality of those remaining in the pool diminishes and the percentage of psychos increases.

For those who are in the pool later in life, this book becomes very important. The dating scene will be full of the walking wounded and those personalities who cannot make relationships work. The psychos are more common. Therefore, you need to upskill and be cautious. Do not lose hope as you only need to find one person.

Younger or older, it is critically important to consider your relationship choice as the most important investment you will ever make. Do not do a lucky dip, hoping that the first one who likes you is Mr or Ms Right. You need to actively select the person with whom you will spend your life.

I will state again that a good relationship is the happiest place on earth, a mediocre relationship is like dragging around a millstone, and a bad relationship can be a living hell. Get out if the relationship is physically violent and work your way out if the relationship is psychologically violent. No religion, belief or rule justifies staying in harmful places. You are too special to waste precious days, weeks, months and years of your life. Time has no shelf life and is not reversable. Make the moments count. By the same token, a relationship should not be viewed lightly nor changed in the same way as fashion changes. Experiencing some problems in the relationship should not be used as justification to get out. Make a concerted effort to fix any problems first.

If you are dating and you are not sure, or the person you are with will not commit, then either move forward with the person or move on. Clear the doorway. If someone is blocking the way, someone else cannot walk through. Ultimately it will be you blocking the passage to a better life if you do not clear the doorway. Psychologically we become scared of the unknown, or scared to be alone, so we waste opportunities. Trust that something good will happen.

If you have had bad experiences, it is normal to have concerns and anxiety about what will happen next. Maybe you have become a little lost fearing the implications of what could go wrong. Fear is a protective emotion, designed to keep you safe.

Just as you can become careful around roads after a car nearly hits you, the same applies with relationships. Fear has a purpose, however, excessive or inappropriate fear will cripple you. My advice to you on this is simple – feel the fear and do it anyway. You must overcome the fear and get on with life.

How would I sum up the key messages in this book? I would say that it is worth trying to find a great relationship even if it takes time. I want you to know that while there is no guaranteed method of choosing an ideal partner and avoiding a psycho, you can greatly improve the odds if you use an evidence-based dating format. I hope that these psychological insights will provide you with a better chance of finding your true love and not a psycho, because love is worth it and so are you.

Love Finder Tools:

- If you think you are a little bit psycho, then you have to make sure that you seek help to make you the best person you can be.

- The dating pool is biggest for those aged 18 to 30 years, so get in early and work hard at it. The older you get, the more selective you will have to be because the quality of the pool diminishes, and the number of psychos increases.

- If someone is standing in the doorway, no one else can come in. Either fix the relationship or clear the pathway for someone new to enter. Do not let fear or loneliness waste your life.

www.ingramcontent.com/pod-product-compliance
Lightning Source LLC
Chambersburg PA
CBHW050638300426
44112CB00012B/1856